PENSION FUNDS

An Annotated Bibliography

by

NELS L. GUNDERSON

The Scarecrow Press, Inc.
Metuchen, N.J., & London
1990

British Library Cataloguing-in-Publication data available

Library of Congress Cataloging-in-Publication Data

Gunderson, Nels L.
    Pension funds: an annotated bibliography / by Nels L. Gunderson.
        p.   cm.
    Includes index.
    ISBN 0-8108-2328-4 (alk. paper)
    1. Pension trusts--United States--Bibliography. I. Title.
Z7164.P4G85 1990
[HD7105.45.U6]
016.33125'2'0973--dc20   90-36013

016.331252097.3
G975p

CONTENTS

LIST OF ABBREVIATIONS

APB: Accounting Principles Board
*ERISA: Employer Retirement Income Security Act of 1974
*ERTA: Economic Recovery Act of 1981
FAS: Financial Accounting Standard
FASB: Financial Accounting Standards Board
FERF: Financial Executives Research Foundation
NBER: National Bureau of Economic Research
NRMA: National Retail Merchants Association
PT: Prohibited Transactions
REA: Retirement Equity Act of 1984
ROI: Return on Investment.
SEPPAA: Single-Employer Pension Plan Amendments Act of 1986
SFAS: Statement of Financial Accounting Standards
SBA: Small Business Administration
SBIC: Small Business Investment Companies
*TEFRA: Tax Equity and Fiscal Responsibility Act of 1982

---

*These acronyms are explained in the Glossary of Terms

INTRODUCTION

This bibliography is intended to aid librarians, students, researchers, and financial managers and executives in locating books, articles, directories, dissertations, and studies on pensions in the United States. Analytical, scholarly, and descriptive journal articles and books from the last 35 to 40 years have been selectively included. Bibliographic citations were compiled from business, public administration, and financial indexes in an effort to include an extensive series of relevant material. Business Periodical Index, ABI/INFORM on-line, the InFoTrac C/D index, Public Affairs Information Service Bulletin, Dissertation Abstracts International, the holdings of the Indiana University Libraries, the Research Libraries Information Network (RLIN) on-line catalog, and other bibliographies were used in the book's compilation.

Many of the works cited in this bibliography are theoretical in content; others examine the policy issues and problems commonly encountered by pension administrators and fiduciaries in the course of investing and managing pension capital. All monographic entries are annotated. Most of the works cited are commercially published and available in academic libraries with business, economics, or public policy collections.

Materials cited in the bibliography were assigned to one of 29 appropriate subject categories. These subject headings reflect the nature of the literature and the important facets of pension management and investment. An author index completes the work.

Nels L. Gunderson
Indiana University
Bloomington, Indiana
April 1990

ACCOUNTING STANDARDS AND PRACTICES

1. "Accounting for Pensions: Longstanding Practice Dumped in Statement No. 87 / . New Accounting Standard for Defined Benefit Plans Described as 'Funny Numbers' by Critics." Employee Benefit Plan Review 40 (March 1986): 10-12, 14-15.

2. Accounting for Pensions; Results of Applying the FASB's Preliminary Views. New York: Coopers & Lybrand, 1983. 256p.
   A research study which considers the potential effects of a single actuarial cost method on the determination of pension expenses. A special amortization method for plan amendments, changes in actuarial assumptions, and actuarial gains or losses are among the areas discussed. Supporting statistical data and plan characteristics are included.

3. Accounting for the Cost of Pension Plans; Text and Explanatory Comments on APB Opinion No. 8. New York: American Institute of Certified Public Accountants, 1968. 109p.
   Pre-ERISA auditing and accounting pension guide.
   A glossary of terms and a selected bibliography are provided.

4. Alldis, Mark C. "Accounting for Pensions: Response to the FASB." Cost & Management 55 (November/December 1981): 53-56.

5. Arcady, Alex T., and Burns, Gary W. "Accounting Rules for Pension Plans: FASB Statements No. 35 and 36." Compensation and Benefit Review 13 (Third Quarter 1981): 39-45.

6. Audits of Employee Benefit Plans. New York: American
    Institute of Certified Public Accountants, 1983. 184p.
    This guide is designed to assist independent auditors
    in interpreting those accounting rules affecting defined
    benefit and defined contribution pension plans. An
    explanation of reporting requirements and regulations
    is provided. Includes footnoted references, a topical
    index, and glossary of terms.

7. Baker, Leroy E. "Accounting for Pension Costs; An
    Historical Survey." Ph.D. dissertation, Harvard Univer-
    sity, 1962.

8. Bassett, P. C. "Who, What and When of Accounting and
    Reporting for Pension Plans." Financial Executive 44
    (January 1976): 12-17.

9. Beresford, Dennis R., and Neary, Robert D. "Accounting
    for Pensions--Two Key Areas." FE: The Magazine for
    Financial Executives 2 (September 1986): 6-10.

10. Beresford, Dennis R., and Neary, Robert D. "Over-
    funded Pension Plans: Assessing Your Alternatives (Part
    1)." FE: The Magazine for Financial Executives 1 (May
    1985): 5-7.

11. Berliner, Robert W., and Gerboth, Dale L. "Accounting
    for Pensions--New FASB Statements." CPA Journal 56
    (April 1986): 12-23.

12. Brown, Betty C., and Coppage, Richard E. "The New
    Employer Pension Standard." National Public Accountant
    31 (September 1986): 26-27.

13. Brownlee, E. Richard, II, and Young, S. David. "Pen-
    sion Accounting: A New Proposal." CPA Journal 55
    (July 1985): 28-34.

14. Buxbaum, William E. "Accounting for Pensions." Manage-
    ment Accounting 65 (October 1983): 24-29.

15. Buxbaum, William E. "Accounting for Pensions: A CFO's
    Views." Journal of Accountancy 156 (December 1983):
    108-114.

16. Christensen, Kenneth E. "The New Pension Accounting." Retail Control 53 (December 1985): 2-24.

17. Cohen, Sheryl L. "Pension Expense Drops 51%." Pensions & Investment Age 15 (July 1987): 2, 40-41, 48.

18. "Complying with ERISA: A Systems Approach." Journal of Accountancy 141 (April 1976): 59-64.

19. Cramer, Joe J., Jr. "Accounting and Reporting Requirements of the Private Pension Trust." DBA dissertation, Indiana University, 1963. 182p.

20. Cropsey, Betsy H. "The Pension Accounting Controversy." Compensation and Benefit Review 16 (Second Quarter 1984): 24-38.

21. Daley, Lane Alan. "The Valuation of Reported Pension Measures for Firms Sponsoring Defined Benefit Plans." Accounting Review 59 (April 1984): 177-198.

22. Dankner, Harold. Accounting for Pensions: Results of Applying the FASB's Preliminary Views. Morristown, NJ: FERF, 1983. 256p.

23. Dankner, Harold. "FASB Issues Final Statement on Pension Accounting--FASB Statement Nos. 87 and 88." Corporate Accounting 4 (Fall 1986): 73-76.

24. Dankner, Harold, and Akresh, Murray. "FASB Issues Exposure Draft on Employers' Accounting for Plan Terminations, Settlements, and Curtailments." Corporate Accounting 4 (Winter 1986): 78-80.

25. Dankner, Harold, and Johnson, Roger. "SFAS no. 87--Employers' Accounting for Pensions." Corporate Accounting 4 (Summer 1986): 83-87.

26. Deitrick, J. W., and Alderman, C. W. "Pension Plans: What Companies Do--And Do Not--Disclose." Management Accounting 61 (April 1980): 24-29.

27. Engstrom, John H. "Pension Reporting by Municipalities." Journal of Accounting, Auditing & Finance 7 (Spring 1984): 197-211.

28. Farney, Kathleen. Collective Bargaining Implications of the FASB Proposals on Pension Accounting. Brookfield, WI: International Foundation of Employee Benefit Plans, 1984. 17p.

29. "FAS No. 88: Accounting for Plan Curtailments and Reversions." Employee Benefit Plan Review 40 (March 1986): 12-13.

30. "FASB Proposes New Pension Plan Standards." CA Magazine 112 (September 1979): 14-15.

31. Feldtmose, J. N., and Roenisch, D. H. "FASB Statement on Defined Benefit Plans: Stop or Go?" Pension World 13 (September 1977): 42-45.

32. Financial Accounting Standards Board. Accounting and Reporting by Defined Benefit Pension Plans. Stamford, CT: The Board, 1980. 145p.

33. Financial Accounting Standards Board. Deferral of the Effective Date of Certain Accounting Requirements for Pension Plans of State and Local Governmental Units: An Amendment of FASB Statement no. 35. Stamford, CT: The Board, 1983. 4p.

34. Financial Accounting Standards Board. Disclosure of Pension Information: An Amendment of APB Opinion no. 8. Stamford, CT: The Board, 1980. 11p.

35. Financial Accounting Standards Board. Employers' Accounting for Settlements and Curtailments of Defined Benefit Pension Plans and for Termination Benefits. Stamford, CT: The Board, 1985. 43p.

36. Flegm, Eugene H. "Pension Accounting--The Search for 'Truth'." Corporate Accounting 2 (Summer 1984): 30-38.

37. Fratar, T., and Gilbert, B. "Pension Cost Accounting and the Implications of Unfunded Vested Liabilities for Financial Statement Analysis." Journal of Commercial Bank Lending 59 (July 1977): 32-44.

38. Freeman, Robert J., and Shoulders, Craig D. "Disclosures for Government Pension Plans." Government Accountants Journal 36 (Summer 1987): 60-62.

39. Ghicas, Dimitrios C. "An Analysis of the Change of
    Actuarial Cost Methods for Pension Accounting and
    Funding." Ph.D. dissertation, University of Florida,
    1985. 127p.

40. Gibson, K. P. "FASB's Proposal on Accounting and Re-
    porting by Defined Benefit Pension Plans: A Hindrance
    or a Help?" Financial Executive 47 (December 1979):
    48-53.

41. Gilbert, Geoffrey M. Accounting and Auditing for Em-
    ployee Benefit Plans. Boston: Warren, Gorham & Lamont,
    1978. 450p.
    This well-organized work, intended for auditors,
    examines reporting requirements for pensions, in-
    cluding defined benefit and defined contribution
    plans among others. The Employment Retirement In-
    come Security Act, Internal Revenue Code qualifications,
    acturial valuation methods, and FASB and AICPA
    guidelines are among the key areas outlined.

42. Gropper, Diane H. "Pensions: How Damaging Will the
    New Accounting Laws BE?" Institutional Investor 20
    (April 1986): 131-142.

43. Harrold, Steven, et al. "How Much Do Pensions Really
    Cost?--Accounting Views from the USA, UK & Canada."
    Benefits International 12 (May 1983): 2-11.

44. Haugh, James W. "New Rules for Pension Accounting
    (Part 1)." Magazine of Bank Administration 62 (May
    1986): 4-10.

45. Hooks, Karen L. "Accounting for Pensions." Woman CPA
    48 (April 1986): 32-33.

46. Javits, J. K. "Pension Reform and the Accountant."
    New York Certified Public Accountant 41 (December 1971):
    929+.

47. Jenkins, D. O. "Accounting for Funded Industrial
    Pension Plans." Accounting Review 39 (July 1964):
    648-653.

48. Klein, John R. "FASB Pension Standards--Views on Im-
    plementation." Ohio CPA Journal 45 (Summer 1986): 61-65.

49. Kline, Allan M., and Fetters, Michael. "The New Pension Accounting." Massachusetts CPA Review 57 (Summer 1983): 22-31.

50. Kreiser, L. "New Accounting Model for Pension Costs." CPA 45 (June 1975): 37-41.

51. Landsman, Wayne. "An Empirical Investigation of Pension Fund Property Rights." Accounting Review 61 (October 1986): 662-691.

52. Lavin, William K. "NRMA Testimony Before the Financial Accounting Standards Board on Employer Accounting for Pensions and Other Postemployment Benefits." Retail Control 52 (February 1984): 39-45.

53. Liebtag. Bill. "Accounting for Pensions." Journal of Accountancy 161 (April 1986): 53-57.

54. Lucas, Timothy S. "How the FASB Views Pension Accounting." Financial Executive 51 (September 1983): 42-51.

55. Malmon, A. S. "Pension Plan Contributions." Journal of Accountancy 109 (June 1960): 56-59.

56. Maloney, Elizabeth. "Will Pension Liabilities Hurt Corporate Balance Sheets?" Institutional Investor 17 (October 1983): 219-224.

57. Means, Kathryn M. "The New Pension Statement: Guide to Application." Woman CPA 49 (January 1987): 3-8.

58. Mielke, David E. "A Pension Decision Model for the Employer." Decision Sciences 17 (Fall 1986): 558-571.

59. Miller, Paul B. W. "The New Pension Accounting (Part 1)." Journal of Accountancy 163 (January 1987): 98-198.

60. Miller, Paul B. W. "The New Pension Accounting (Part 2): Putting It into Practice." Journal of Accountancy 163 (February 1987): 86-94.

61. Morris, Michael H., and Nichols, William D. "Pension

Accounting and the Balance Sheet: The Potential Effect
of the FASB's Preliminary Views." Journal of Accounting,
Auditing & Finance 7 (Summer 1984):   293-305.

62. Morris, William J., Jr.   "Accounting for Common Stocks
for Church Pension Funds--An Empirical Evaluation."
Ph.D. dissertation, Michigan State University, 1971.
210p.

63. Murray, Ronald J., and Decker, William E.   "Implementing
the New Pension Accounting Rules." Journal of Compensation & Benefits 2 (January/February 1987):   249-252.

64. Murray, Ronald J., and Decker, William E.   "Transferring
Excess Pension Assets to an ESOP." Journal of Compensation & Benefits 3 (March/April 1988):   314-316.

65. Murray, Ronald J., et al.   "Pension Accounting: Analysis
of 'Preliminary Views'--Part I." CPA Journal 53 (August
1983):   10-23.

66. Murray, Ronald J., et al.   "Pension Accounting: Analysis
of 'Preliminary Views'--Part II." CPA Journal 53 (September 1983):   42-47.

67. Novak, Frank S., and Koeblitz, William M.   "Pensions:
The Surprise Package in Corporate Marriage." Management
Accounting 65 (January 1984):   50-55.

68. Parker, Marcia.   "Managing the Pension Surplus: Latest
FASB Rules Have Execs Looking at Liabilities." Pension
& Investment Age 14 (December 8, 1986):   34.

69. Paustian, Chuck, and Cohen, Sheryl.   "FASB 87 Impact
Puts Pension Executives in Quandary over Strategy."
Pensions & Investment Age 15 (June 1, 1987):   3, 47.

70. "Pension Plan Accounting Can Affect Acquisition Cost."
WG&L Accounting News 8 (Winter 1987):   13-14.

71. Rappaport, Anna M.   "If ERISA Didn't Kill Pensions
FASB May." Office Administration & Automation 44
(February 1983):   37-41, 80.

72. "Results of Pensions Field Test Published." WG&L Accounting News 5 (Spring 1984):   12-15.

73. Ring, Trudy. "Asset-Liability Studies Flourish."
Pensions & Investment Age 15 (July 1987): 2, 38.

74. Rue, Joseph C., and Volkan, Ara G. "Financial and
Economic Consequences of the New Pension Accounting
Proposals: Is the Gloom Justified?" Journal of Accounting,
Auditing & Finance 7 (Summer 1984): 306-322.

75. Seaman, Jerome F., and Hensold, Harold H., Jr. "Pension Plan Obligations: The 'Real' Impact." Journal of
Accountancy 154 (July 1982): 82-88.

76. Shultz, Paul T., and Margel, Lawrence N. "Employers'
Accounting for Pensions: An Analysis of the FASB Ex-
posure Draft and Its Implications." Employee Relations
Law Journal 11 (Autumn 1985): 355-360.

77. Shultz, Paul T., and Woyke, John F. "FAS 87: Employers Accounting for Pensions." Employee Relations Law
Journal 12 (Summer 1986): 153-161.

78. Smith, L. Murphy, and Putnam, Karl B. "Pension Dilemmas: 1. Inflation and Government Rules." Compensation
& Benefits Review 17 (November/December 1985): 16-22.

79. Soosten, D. Von, Jr., and Murphy, G. C. "Must Bank-
Trusteed Employee-Benefit Plans Be Audited?" Financial
Executive 44 (April 1976): 36-39.

80. Stanger, Abraham M. "Accounting for Pension Costs:
Conflict Between Concepts and Standards." Corporation
Law Review 5 (Spring 1982): 180-183.

81. Stewart, John E., and Neuhausen, Benjamin S. "Understanding and Implementing the New Pension Rules."
Corporate Accounting 5 (Winter 1987): 41-50.

82. Stone, Mary S. "The Changing Picture for Pension
Accounting." CPA Journal 53 (April 1983): 32-42.

83. Stone, Mary [S.], and Bublitz, Bruce. "An Analysis of the
Reliability of the FASB Date Bank of Changing Price and
Pension Information." Accounting Review 59 (July 1984):
469-473.

84. Todd, Terrye A., and Posey, Clyde L. "Adequate Disclosure of Pension Liabilities: A Survey of Executive Opinion." Mid-South Business Journal 6 (July 1986): 22-26.

85. Waggoner, Sharon S. "Pension Accounting: The Liability Controversy." Management Accounting 67 (July 1985): 54-57.

86. Walker, David M. "Accounting for Reversions from Pension Plans." Journal of Accountancy 159 (February 1985): 64-70.

87. Wallis, Charles T. "FASB Statement No. 87 and the Bottom Line." Corporate Accounting 5 (Fall 1987): 38-41.

88. Walsh, Francis J. New Rules for Pension Accounting. New York: Conference Board, 1983. 15p.
    A brief overview of accounting procedures which summarizes and examines Financial Accounting Standards Board proposals.

89. Ward, Graham. "Pension Fund Reporting--An International Comparison." Benefits & Compensation International 17 (July 1987): 16-24.

90. Welsh, Mary J., and Trapnell, Jerry E. "Labor Market Models and Employer Accounting for Pensions." Journal of Accounting, Auditing & Finance 8 (Winter 1985): 100-111.

91. Werner, Charles A., and Kostolansky, John W. "Accounting Liabilities Under ERISA." Journal of Accounting, Auditing & Finance 7 (Fall 1983): 54-64.

92. White, Gerald I. "Pension Accounting: A Challenge for the FASB." Corporate Accounting 2 (Spring 1984): 4-12.

93. Zorn, Paul. "Public Pension Funding: Preliminary Results from a Survey of Current Practices." Government Finance Review 3 (August 1987): 7-11.

94. Bell, Donald, and Hill, Diane. "How Social Security Payments Affect Private Pensions." Monthly Labor Review 107 (May 1984): 15-20.

95. Bristol, James T. "Integrating Pension Plans with Social Security." Arkansas Business & Economic Review 18 (1985): 6-14.

96. Cohen, Cynthia F. "The Impact on Women of Proposed Changes in the Private Pension System: A Simulation." Industrial & Labor Relations Review 36 (January 1983): 258-270.

97. Cook, Thomas J. "What Employers Are Saying About Lump-Sum Distributions." Pension World 20 (June 1984): 45-48.

98. Davis, H. E. "Growth of Benefits in a Cohort of Pension Plans." Monthly Labor Review 94 (May 1971): 46-50.

99. Ferguson, William A. "Pension 'Nuggets' Combine the Best of Both Worlds." Pension World 21 (July 1985): 44-46.

100. Greene, M. R. "Effect of Pension Provisions on Employment of Older Persons." CLU Journal 34 (July 1980): 63-69.

101. Heaton, Herbert. "An Indexed Pension Plan at Low Cost." Pension World 11 (September 1975): 43-44.

102. Johnson, Warren A. "Inflation-Proof Pension Plans." Best's Review Life and Health Insurance Edition 84 (November 1983): 22-25, 120-122.

103. Kittrell, Alison. "Retirement Benefits Survey: Defined Benefit Plan Top Choice / Defined Contribution Plans Gain Popularity." Business Insurance 21 (August 1987): 28-30.

104. Laketek, Maryann. "Employee Benefits: Four Reasons to Rethink Your Retirement Benefits." Cash Flow 8 (July 1987): 30-34.

105. McGill, Dan Preservation of Pension Benefit Rights. Homewood, IL: Richard D. Irwin, Inc., 1972. 382p. This treatise summarizes the public policy implications of mandatory and voluntary pension vesting. Reciprocity agreements, the cost of vesting, and the mechanisms for implementing benefit plans are among the topics explored. Statistical tables and footnoted references are included.

106. Misher, Norman J. "Recent Developments in Employee Benefits: Plan Distribution Developments." Journal of Pension Planning & Compliance 12 (Spring 1986): 51-56.

107. Nader, Ralph, and Blackwell, Kate. You and Your Pension. New York: Grossman, 1973. 215p. This provocative work is intended to help employees exert influence over management and government in an attempt to receive equitable pension benefits. Explanations of federal legislative proposals from the 1970s, which were designed to improve the private pension system, are presented.

108. Oliver, William G. "Partnership Shapes Progress in Benefits Education." Pension World 14 (September 1978): 10-12.

109. Paul, Robert D. "Evolutionary Trends in Benefit Design." Pension World 20 (April 1984): 23-26.

110. Paustian, Chuck. "Benefit Payments Top Contributions." Pensions & Investment Age 15 (January 26, 1987): 15, 77.

111. Pesando, James E. "Employee Evaluation of Pension Claims and the Impact of Indexing Initiatives." Economic Inquiry 22 (January 1984): 1-17.

112.   Rakowski, Ronald J.   "Lump-Sum Distribution: A
       Word of Caution for the Highly Compensated." Pension
       World 18 (March 1982):   46-48.

113.   Rosenbaum, William C., Jr.   "The Pension Swindle."
       Association Management 37 (October 1985):   107-108.

114.   Schmitt, Donald G.   "Today's Pension Plans: How Much
       Do They Pay?" Monthly Labor Review 108 (December
       1985):   19-25.

115.   Schulz, James H., et al.   "The Incidence of Integration
       Provisions in Private Pension Plans." Journal of Pension
       Planning & Compliance 9 (October 1983):   399-407.

116.   Schulz, James H., and Leavit, Thomas D.   Pension
       Integration: Concepts, Issues and Proposals.   Washing-
       ton, DC: Employee Benefit Research Institute, 1983.
       83p.
            This study examines the coordination of pension
       plan benefits with social security payments.   Inte-
       gration related concepts, terms, and procedures are
       discussed in some detail.   The effect of integration
       on retirement income levels and pension plan costs
       is also ascertained.

117.   Stiteler, Allen.   "Finally, Pension Plans Defined."
       Personnel Journal 66 (February 1987):   44-53.

118.   "What Benefits 21 Million Workers Receive." Employee
       Benefit Plan Review 40 (October 1985):   48-56.

CASH BALANCE PLANS

119. "Bank America Begins Cash Balance Pension Plan."
     Employee Benefit Plan Review 40 (November 1985):
     106-108.

120. "Best of Both Worlds in Cash Balance Pension Plan."
     Employee Benefit Plan Review 40 (November 1985): 52-
     53.

121. Brennan, Lawrence T. "Achieving the Best of Both
     Worlds with a Cash Balance Pension Plan." Journal of
     Compensation & Benefits 1 (November/December 1985):
     133-139.

122. Geisel, Jerry. "Use of Pension Hybrid Expected to
     Grow." Business Insurance 19 (August 26, 1985):
     3-4, 8.

123. Perham, John C. "New Design in Pensions." Dun's
     Business Month 127 (January 1986): 70-72.

124. Tokerud, Douglas. "New on the Pension Scene: The
     Cash-Balance Plan." Compensation & Benefits Review
     18 (January/February 1986): 33-42.

125. Bodie, Zvi. Defined Benefit Versus Defined Contribution
      Pension Plans. Cambridge, MD: National Bureau of
      Economic Research, 1985. 35p.
      This technical paper examines the major financial
      factors to be considered when choosing between de-
      fined benefit and defined contribution pension plans.
      The advantages, disadvantages, and risks associated
      with each plans funding and investment strategy are
      analyzed. Includes annotated footnotes, supporting
      statistical tables, and benefit formulas.

126. Crosby, William M. "An Examination of the Effects Which
      a Change in the Interest Rate Has on Pension Costs
      and Liabilities in Companies with Defined Benefit Pension
      Plans." Ph.D. dissertation, University of Georgia,
      1985. 159p.

127. Daley, Lane A. "The Valuation of Reported Pension
      Measures for Firms Sponsoring Defined Benefit Plans."
      Ph.D. dissertation, University of Washington, 1982.
      297p.

128. Ellig, Bruce R. "Defined-Benefit Retirement Annuities:
      Testing Competitiveness." Compensation Review 14
      (Fourth Quarter 1982): 14-29.

129. Graves, Thomas C. "Recapture of Surplus Defined
      Benefit Plan Assets from an Ongoing Program: PBGC,
      IRS and DOL Guidelines." Journal of Pension Planning
      & Compliance 10 (August 1984): 267-274.

130. Guardino, Joseph R. "Top Heavy Pension and Profit
      Sharing Plans Post TEFRA." National Public Accountant
      29 (August 1984): 50-51, 53.

131. Holland, Rodger G., and Sutton, Nancy A. "The
     Liability Nature of Unfunded Pension Obligations Since
     ERISA." Journal of Risk & Insurance 55 (March
     1988): 32-58.

132. Kemp, Robert S., et al. "An Analysis of the Investment
     Decision of Defined Benefit Pension Funds from the
     Corporate Perspective." Benefits Quarterly 2 (First
     Quarter 1986): 18-25.

133. Kittrell, Alison. "Recapturing Assets--Pension Surplus
     Belongs to Employers: Survey." Business Insurance
     18 (July 9, 1984): 1, 30-31.

134. Lang, Larry. "Defined Benefit, Defined Contribution:
     Which One's Better?" Pension World 22 (October 1986):
     28-32.

135. Logue, Dennis E. Legislative Influence on Corporate
     Pension Plans. Washington, DC: American Enterprise
     Institute for Public Policy Research, 1979. 109p.
     An examination of the future of defined benefit
     plans offered by large corporations. The integration
     of social security benefits and private pension plans
     is discussed. Includes a summary of ERISA's major
     provisions.

136. Mara, Rod. "The Exciting New Pension Message of
     PERC." Journal of Compensation & Benefits 1 (November/
     December 1985): 177-179.

137. Pelletier, A. David. "Defined Benefit Vs. Defined
     Contribution Plans in Uncertain Economic Environments."
     Benefits & Compensation International 15 (December 1985):
     15-18.

138. "Pension Field Concern: Excess Assets, Plan Design."
     Employee Benefit Plan Review 41 (October 1986): 40-44.

139. Ring, Trudy. "Portfolio Insurance Is Gaining Exposure."
     Pensions & Investment Age 14 (December 8, 1986):
     15, 29.

140. Rizzuto, Paul A. "Pension Dilemmas: 2. Restructuring
     Pensions in a Volatile Environment." Compensation &
     Benefits Review 17 (November/December 1985): 23-37.

141. Shapiro, Kenneth P. "Shrunken Assets: Pension Plans
      Amidst Market Turmoil." Directors & Boards 12 (Winter
      1988): 29-30.

142. Tatge, David B. "Preparing for Excess Asset Reversions
      on Termination of Defined-Benefit Plans." Journal of
      Taxation 63 (July 1985): 20-25.

DEFINED CONTRIBUTION PLANS

143. Christman, Ed, et al. "Defined Contribution Plans:
      Fund Execs Trade Investing for Paper Work/Insurers,
      Banks Find New Business." Pensions & Investment Age
      13 (November 11, 1985): 37, 42-43, 47.

144. Davies, J. J. "Defined Contribution Plan Management."
      Pension World 15 (June 1979): 60-62.

145. Donahue, Richard J. "Defined Contribution Plans Lead."
      National Underwriter (Property/Casualty/Employee
      Benefits) 91 (May 4, 1987): 3, 55.

146. Jones, Michael B. "Making the Switch to a Defined
      Contribution Plan." Journal of Compensation & Benefits
      1 (January/February 1986): 220-222.

147. Moreen, Robert A. "Why Choose a Defined Contribution
      Plan?" Pension World 21 (January 1985): 46-49.

148. Pitkofsky, Gary R. "Defined Contribution Plan Re-
      views Start with the Basics." Pension World 21 (Novem-
      ber 1985): 46-49.

149. Spencer, Ross D. "Defined Contribution Plans Have
      Valuable Benefit Roles but Should Not Replace Defined
      Benefit Plans." Employee Benefit Plan Review 39 (March
      1985): 38-42.

150. Directory of Pension Funds and Their Investment
     Managers. Charlottesville, VA: Money Market Director-
     ies, 1983-   (Annual).
     This work provides information on 24,000 organizations
     that sponsor over one million in tax-exempt assets.
     Directory coverage includes over 50,000 pension and
     profit-sharing plans in the United States.

151. Financial Directory of Pension Funds. Washington,
     DC: ERISA Benefit Funds, Inc. (Irregular).
     An excellent guide which identifies corporate and
     union, defined benefit and defined contribution pen-
     sion funds by location, employee size, type of plan,
     and asset value. A list of Keogh plans is also in-
     cluded with similar information. Volumes are organ-
     ized by state and/or region.

152. Allen, Steven G., et al. Job Mobility, Older Workers
      and the Role of Pensions. Raleigh: North Carolina
      State University, 1986. 106p.
      This study attempts to determine, through numerical
      analysis, the magnitude of pension-related incentives
      that discourage job mobility. The estimation of job
      change and length of tenure equations are calculated
      using compiled time series data. The work's appendi-
      ces include mathematical derivations, a bibliography,
      and supporting statistical data.

153. Burkhauser, Richard V. "The Early Pension Decision
      and Its Effect on Exit from the Labor Market." Ph.D.
      dissertation, University of Chicago, 1976.

154. Clark, Arben O. "Employee Perception of and Attitude
      Toward the Pension Plans of Employing Organizations."
      DBA dissertation, Indiana University, 1963. 171p.

155. Douthitt, Robin A. "Pension Information and the Retire-
      ment Decision of Married Women." Ph.D. dissertation,
      Cornell University, 1982. 120p.

156. "Finances, Employee Morale in Acquisition Talks."
      Employee Benefit Plan Review 42 (March 1988): 34-35.

157. Ford, Gary R. "Statewide Assessment Survey of
      Michigan Public School Employees Retirement System
      Members to Determine Pension Benefit Awareness."
      Ph.D. dissertation, University of Michigan, 1975. 143p.

19

158. The Annotated Fiduciary: Materials on Fiduciary Responsibility and Prohibited Transactions under ERISA.
Brookfield, WI: International Foundation of Employee Benefit Plans, 1980. 487p.
A compendium of ERISA provisions, regulations, and interpretive bulletins. Synopses of relevant court decisions are provided.

159. Gertner, Marc. "ERISA in Retrospect." Journal of Pension Planning & Compliance 10 (August 1984): 275-296.

160. Myers, Donald J., and Curto, Michael A. "Fiduciary Duties Under ERISA." Compensation & Benefits Mgmt 4 (Spring 1988): 199-206.

FIDUCIARY RESPONSIBILITY/LIABILITY

161. Betterley, Delbart A. "You Can Protect Yourself from Fiduciary Responsibility." Pension World 13 (May 1977): 41-44.

162. Burroughs, Eugene B. "Professionalism Begets Professionalism." Pension World 20 (July 1984): 57, 60.

163. Hirzel, Patrick S., and Mamorsky, Jeffrey D. "Fiduciary Audits: Defusing the Pension Time Bomb." Corporate Accounting 1 (Winter 1983): 60-63.

164. Hutchinson, James D. "The Compleat Fiduciary." Pension World 14 (April 1978): 45-60.

165. Mamorsky, J[effrey] D., and Cleveland, M. G. "Solving Fiduciary Responsibility Questions in Collectively Bargained Plans." Pension World 15 (February 1979): 61-64+.

166. Mamorsky, Jeffrey D., and Rasmussen, Eva A. "What Every Fiduciary Should Know." Pension World 19 (January 1983): 57-59.

167. Pianko, Howard. "Plan Investments & Fiduciary Liability." Journal of Pension Planning & Compliance 11 (Fall 1985): 241-249.

168. Plutchok, Jonathan. "On Pensions: Fiduciary Blues." Financial Planning 15 (February 1986): 186-188.

169. Ring, Trudy. "Some Plans Limited on Liability Coverage." Pension & Investment Age 15 (January 26, 1987): 3, 89.

170. Roskopf, John. "Designing Fiduciary Liability Protection." Cash Flow 9 (April 1988): 28-34.

171. Weiss, R. L., and Voboril, J. S. "Fiduciary Standards
      and Investment Responsibility Under the New Pension
      Reform Law." Trusts & Estates 113 (December 1974):
      800-803+.

172. Abbott, R. W. "Industry and the State Pension Scheme." Personnel Management 42 (June 1960): 108-114.

173. Allen, Everett T., Jr., et al. Pension Planning: Pensions, Profit Sharing and Other Deferred Compensation Plans. 5th ed. Homewood, IL: Richard D. Irwin, Inc., 1984. 448p.
   This comprehensive textbook, intended for upper-level college students, covers a wide range of pension-related topics. Plan funding, pension benefits, self-employed plans, ERISA, and relevant IRS disclosure requirements are several of the areas covered.

174. Andrews, Emily S. The Changing Profile of Pensions in America. Washington, DC: Employee Benefit Research Institute, 1985. 234p.
   This substantive overview of the retirement income system examines current trends in employer-sponsored pensions and the relationship between industry growth, the business cycle, and pension plan coverage. The impact of the Retirement Equity Act on pension plan costs is also assessed. Includes explanatory references, supporting statistical appendices, and income policy proposals.

175. Background Analysis of the Potential Effects of a Minimum Universal Pension System: Final Report Submitted to the President's Commission on Pension Policy and ... the Department of Labor. Washington, DC: ICF Inc., 1981. Various pagings.
   This report assesses the probable impact of a universal pension system on the economy, employment, and personal savings in the United States. The possible

effects of a minimum universal pension plan on retirement benefit costs, participation and vesting, and
benefit receipt are also investigated. Includes supporting statistical data, explanatory references, and
a chapter on policy alternatives.

176. Bartell, Harry R., Jr. "Unions and Pension Funds."
Ph.D. dissertation, Columbia University, 1963.

177. Batten, Michael D., and French, Julia R. "Are Employers and Older Workers at the Crossroads?" Pension
World 14 (November 1978): 10-16.

178. Beattie, O. C., and Brothers, D. I. "Pension Funds
and the Winds of Change." Financial Executive 35 (March
1967): 24+.

179. Bodie, Zvi, ed. Pensions in the U.S. Economy. Chicago:
University of Chicago Press, 1988. 200p.
An excellent collection of papers presented at the
1985 NBER conference which examine pension plan
funding and the relationship between pension plan
coverage and employee turnover. Professors Robert
C. Merton, Michael J. Boskin, Edward P. Lazear,
and Steven Venti are several of the conferees whose
papers appear in the volume. Includes subject and
author indexes.

180. Bodie, Zvi; Shoven, John B.; and Wise, David A.,
eds. Issues in Pension Economics. Chicago: University
of Chicago Press, 1987. 376p.
A collection of papers presented at a 1984 NBER
Conference which explore corporate pension policy,
unfunded pension liabilities, pension inequalities, and
pension plan integration. Michael J. Boskin, Alan
J. Marcus, R. Gleen Hubbard, and Jeremy I. Bulow
are among the conferees contributing to this volume.
Includes actuarial formulas and supporting demographic
data.

181. Bristol, James T. "A Pension Plan Primer." Arkansas
Business & Economic Review 16 (1938): 10-17.

182. Burianek, Frank. "Pension Plans--Is the Sky Really
Falling?" Pension World 14 (February 1978): 6-14.

183. Chia, Nelson P. "Simplifying the Pension Plan." Life
      Association News 78 (January 1983): 104-109.

184. Cooper, Robert D. Pension Fund Operations and Ex-
      penses: The Technical Report. Brookfield, WI: Inter-
      national Foundation of Employee Benefit Plans, 1980.
      149p.
      A study which analyzes collectively bargained, multi-
      employer defined benefit plans and their operational
      costs. Annual employer contribution figures, ag-
      gregate plan assets, and operational costs are sur-
      veyed. Statistical tables, IRS pension schedules,
      and a sample of the study's questionnaire are pro-
      vided.

185. Croot, D. J. "Worlds in Collision; Pensions, Social
      Security, and Welfare." Financial Executive 41 (May
      1973): 70-72+.

186. Dearing, Charles L. Industrial Pensions. Washington,
      DC: Brookings Institution, 1954. 310p.
      A timely study which attempts to determine whether
      pension obligations can be met by industry without
      placing undue burdens upon wage-earners and stock-
      holders. Pension fund investment, plus the amount
      and nature of pension plan contributions, is also
      discussed. Includes statistical tables and applicable
      sections of the IRS tax code.

187. Drucker, Peter F. The Unseen Revolution: How Pension
      Fund Socialism Came to America. New York: Harper
      & Row, 1976. 214p.
      This provocative book assesses the social, economic,
      political, and demographic factors that have contri-
      buted to the growth of pension funds in the United
      States. The future of the social security system
      and the effects of pension fund growth on private
      enterprise and ownership are considered. Includes
      an informative section on population dynamics, birth-
      rates, and dependency ratios.

188. Dungan, V. L. "What Do the Elections Mean to the
      Pension World?" Pension World 17 (January 1981):
      20-24.

189. Ehrbar, A. F. "Those Pension Plans Are Even Weaker
     Than You Think." Fortune 96 (November 1977): 104-
     108+.

190. Ellis, C. D. "Danger Ahead for Pension Funds."
     Harvard Business Review 49 (May 1971): 50-56.

191. Employee Retirement Systems: How It All Began."
     Pension World 12 (July 1976): 6-8+.

192. Finston, Irving L. Pension Funds and Insurance Re-
     serves. Homewood, IL: Dow Jones-Irwin, 1986. 229p.
     An examination of the insurance industry's manage-
     ment and investment of private pension funds. The
     various types of financial practices associated with
     formula contribution plans are briefly explored.

193. Garfin, Louis. "On Pension Fund Reserves." Ph.D.
     dissertation, University of Iowa, 1942.

194. Gilbert, Lewis D. "It's Time for Pension Democracy."
     Pension World 13 (November 1977): 33-36.

195. Givens, Harrison, Jr. "How Pension Plans Can Cope
     with Inflation." Pension World 12 (June 1976): 37-42.

196. Greenough, William C., and King, Francis P. Pension
     Plans and Public Policy. New York: Columbia Univer-
     sity Press, 1976. 311p.
     Social security, private pensions, and public employee
     pensions are examined as the three major components
     of the retirement age income support structure.
     Descriptions of the various types of pension plans
     currently in operation and the changes in pension
     investment policies over the last several decades are
     also presented. Includes tables, charts and footnoted
     references.

197. Goodman, Isidore. Integrated Pension and Profit-Sharing
     Plans. Chicago: Commerce Clearing House, 1980. 31p.
     A brief report which outlines the basic requirements
     for establishing flat benefit and unit benefit excess
     plans.

198. Harbrecht, Paul P. "Pension Funds and Economic
      Power." Ph.D. dissertation, Columbia University, 1963.

199. Hennington, Howard H. "Will Inflation Penalize the Re-
      tiree or the Plan Sponsor?" Pension World 13 (March
      1977): 44-49.

200. Horlick, Max. "The Relationships Between Public and
      Private Pension Schemes: An Introductory Overview."
      Social Security Bulletin 50 (July 1987): 15-24.

201. Ippolito, Richard A. Pensions, Economics and Public
      Policy. Homewood, IL: Dow Jones-Irwin, 1986. 267p.
      This provocative study explores pension growth in
      the United States, pension plan characteristics, the
      economic principles of pensions, and the public
      policy implications of taxing private pension plans.
      The impact of pensions on the capital markets is also
      assessed. Includes supporting statistical informaiton,
      a bibliography, and dissenting comments from two
      consultants in the field.

202. Kalish, Gerald I., et al. "Pension & Benefit Perspectives."
      Cash Flow 7 (February 1986): 25-35.

203. Katz, Lawrence G. "Pensions Are a Full Time Commit-
      ment." Life Association News 81 (November 1986): 91-
      95.

204. Kolodrubetz, W. W. "Reciprocity and Pension Portability."
      Monthly Labor Review 91 (September 1968): 22-28.

205. Leibig, Michael T. Social Investments and the Law: The
      Case for Alternative Investments. Washington, DC:
      Conference on Alternative State and Local Policies, 1980.
      79p.
      This work examines the judicial decisions and federal
      statutes which have influenced the investment of
      pension fund capital. The effect of ERISA, the Taft-
      Hartley Act, and the Internal Revenue Code on pension
      fund investment policies are also briefly assessed.
      Applicable fiduciary standards, and footnoted refer-
      ences are cited.

206. Litvak, Lawrence. Pension Funds & Economic Renewal.

Washington, DC: Council of State Planning Agencies,
1981.   141p.
This study considers pension fund investment as a
means to promote job creation, affordable housing
and economic development. The effects of (economic)
development investing on portfolio performance is
assessed. Includes tables, exhibits, and a bibliography.

207.   Main, J. "Building a 21st-Century Pension Right Now."
       Money 5 (September 1976):   38-42.

208.   Munnell, A. H. "Battle of the Heavyweights: Social
       Security Vs. Private Pensions." Pension World 15
       (January 1979):   45-49.

209.   Musick, Robert L., Jr. "Toward a National Pension
       Policy." Journal of Pension Planning & Compliance 10
       (August 1984):   297-309.

210.   Olian, Judy D., et al. "It's Time to Start Using Your
       Pension System to Improve the Bottom Line." Personnel
       Administrator 30 (April 1985):   77-83, 152.

211.   Pension, Profit-Sharing, and Other Deferred Compensation
       Plans. Philadelphia: American Law Institute/American
       Bar Association Committee on Continuing Professional
       Education, 1984-1985.

212.   "Pensions Focus More on Results: LOMA." National
       Underwriter (Life/Health/Financial Services) 91 (January
       12, 1987):   20-22.

213.   Phillips, S. M., and Fletcher, L. P. "Future of the
       Portable Pension Concept." Industrial and Labor Re-
       lations Review 30 (January 1977):   197-203.

214.   Pomeranz, Felix. Pensions: An Accounting and Manage-
       ment Guide. New York: Ronald Press Co., 1976.
       329p.
       This textbook covers the principal provisions of
       ERISA, the basics of pension plan funding, and the
       fundamentals of auditing and financial pension re-
       porting. An excellent chapter on the management
       implications of ERISA is also featured. Includes an
       index of ERISA sections and a selected bibliography.

215. Raskin, A. H. "Pension Power." Journal of the Insti-
      tute for Socioeconomic Studies 6 (Winter 1981/1982):
      76-99.

216. Regan, Patrick J. "Crosscurrents in the Pension
      Picture." Financial Analysts Journal 40 (January/
      February 1984): 15-17.

217. Regan, P[atrick] J. "Is the Pension Burden for American
      Industry Growing?" Financial Analysts Journal 35
      (September 1979): 6-7.

218. Rifkin, Jeremy, and Barber, Randy. The North Will
      Rise Again: Pensions, Power, and Politics in the 1980s.
      Boston: Beacon Press, 1978. 279p.
      A provocative analysis of the social, demographic,
      economic, and political conditions which are affecting
      U.S. pension plan coverage and investment. The
      role of organized labor in the battle over the control
      and use of pension capital is described. Includes
      footnoted references for each chapter.

219. Sahin, Izzet. "Bruce's Spider and the Employee's Risk
      Under a Pension System." Journal of Risk & Insurance
      51 (March 1984): 143-149.

220. Selinske, Charles E. "My Pension Plan is Killing Me!"
      Pension World 11 (June 1975): 21-43.

221. Shapiro, Kenneth P. "An Ideal Pension System."
      Personnel Journal 60 (April 1981): 294-297.

222. Tilove, Robert. Pension Funds and Economic Freedom:
      A Report to the Fund for the Republic. New York:
      Fund for the Republic, 1959. 91p.
      This work examines the effects of private pensions
      on labor mobility in the United States. The potential
      dangers of concentrated power resulting from the
      acquisition of stocks and bonds by pension plans is
      assessed. Includes statistical tables, charts, and
      footnoted references.

223. "Underfunded Plans Threaten Future of All Pensions."
      Employee Benefit Plan Review 42 (July 1987): 46-47.

224. United States. The President's Commission on Pension
      Policy. An Interim Report. Washington, DC: Govern-
      ment Printing Office, 1980. 51p.
          A list of recommendations made by the commission
      which address the issues of retirement income goals,
      the taxation of pension benefits/contributions, the
      employment of older workers, and who maintains
      control and ownership of pension fund assets. An
      executive summary, biographies of the commissioners,
      and a commission fact sheet are included in the re-
      port's appendices.

225. Watson, Harry. "A Note on Pensions in a Neoclassical
      Model of the Firm." Journal of Economic Dynamics &
      Control 6 (September 1983): 41-54.

226. Williams, W. "Value of Pension Promises and Consumer
      Wealth." Journal of Finance 20 (March 1965): 36-48.

227. Wise, David A., ed. Pensions, Labor and Individual
      Choice. Chicago: University of Chicago Press, 1985.
      453p.
          This edited collection of essays and commentaries
      examines the determinants of pension benefits, the
      riskiness of private pensions, and the relationship
      between wages and benefits. Paul A. Samuelson,
      Edward P. Lazear, W. Kip Viscisi, and Robert C.
      Merton are several of the work's distinguished con-
      tributors. Includes tables, mathematical formulas,
      and bibliographic references.

228. Wishart, R. A. "Portability of Pensions." Best's
      Insurance News (Life Edition) 64 (April 1964): 18+.

229. Wyatt Company. "Defined Benefit Plans That Look Like
      Defined Contribution Plans." Personnel Journal 65
      (February 1986): 103-109.

230. Young, Sheldon M. Pension and Profit Sharing Plans.
      New York: Matthew Bender & Co., Inc., 1979- .

GUARANTEED INVESTMENT CONTRACTS

231. Allen, John W. "Six Trends in GICs." Pension World 23 (July 1987): 22-23.

232. Darby, Rose. "$26.9 Billion Held in GICs." Pensions & Investment Age 14 (January 6, 1986): 3, 36.

233. Grennwald, Judy. "Benefit Planning: GIC Market More Than $150 Billion." Business Insurance 22 (May 30, 1988): 3, 10-12.

234. Haggerty, Alfred G. "GICs Survive Tax Reform, Rate Dive." National Underwriter 91 (April 27, 1987): 16-17.

235. Martini, Judith A. "A Guide to GICs." Best's Review Life and Health Insurance Edition 86 (February 1986): 78-82.

236. Mattera, James T. "How to Teach an Old GIC New Tricks." Pension World 22 (February 1986): 30-32, 45.

237. Schmidt, Ned W. "Guaranteed Investment Contracts: From Passive to Active." Pension World 23 (March 1987): 48, 51.

238. Selby, Beth. "Pension Management: The GIC Battle Heats Up." Institutional Investor 20 (May 1986): 105-114.

239. Williams, Fred. "Indexed GICs Attracting New Attention." Pensions & Investment Age 15 (September 1987): 4.

240. Wims, Mary E. "Guaranteed Investment Contracts: Considerations for the Pension Fiduciary." Employee Benefits Journal 8 (June 1983): 5-9.

LAWS AND REGULATIONS

241. Abramson, Stephen, and Mattera, S. George. "Top-Heavy Plans: Insights and Ideas." Journal of Pension Planning & Compliance 10 (February 1984): 21-35.

242. Alberding, R. J. "Communicating Employee Benefits Under ERISA." Financial Executive 43 (July 1975): 42-47.

243. Albert, Rory J., and Schelberg, Neal S. "Controversy Continues Over Excess Pension Plan Asset Reversions." Pension World 23 (May 1987): 42-46, 48.

244. Albert, Rory J., and Schelberg, Neal S. "How OBRA '87 Affects Pension Plans." Pension World 24 (April 1988): 32-37, 46.

245. Alef, D., and Short, G. G. "Problems Created by CA-7 Decision That Pension Plan Participation Is a Security." Journal of Taxation 47 (November 1977): 282-286.

246. Areson, David C., ed. Employee Retirement Income Security Act of 1974, Updated Through September 1, 1986. Paramus, NJ: Prentice-Hall, Inc., 1986. 299p. A full-text amended volume of ERISA accompanied with a comprehensive subject index. Amended sections are footnoted by the publisher.

247. Bader, Lawrence N., and Gagler, Lynda B. "How to Handle the Troublesome Compliance Problems Under the Retirement Equity Act." Practical Accountant 19 (August 1986): 68-78.

248. Baker, Pamela. "Pension Trusts as Limited Partners--Ruminations on UBI and Service Bolt & Nut." Journal of Taxation of Investments 1 (Summer 1984): 348-359.

249. Becker, B. M., and Aronson, A. A. "New Pension Reform Act--What Now? Plan or No Plan." Taxes 54 (January 1976): 36-50.

250. Berger, P. S., and Hester, S. L. "Effect of ERISA on Multi-Employer Plans: Participation, Vesting, Accrual of Benefits." Journal of Taxation 42 (February 1975): 82-86.

251. Bildersee, Robert A. "The Attorney's Role." Pension World 11 (November 1975): 21-26.

252. Blair, R. D. "ERISA and the Prudent Man Rule: Avoiding Perverse Result." Sloan Management Review 20 (Winter 1979): 15-25.

253. Borgmeyer, S. R. "ERISA's Controlled Group Provisions." Pension World 16 (January 1980): 54-56.

254. Brauer, Mary A. "Future Issues in Assessment of Withdrawal Liability Under the Multi-Employer Pension Plan Amendments Act of 1980." Employee Benefits Journal 8 (December 1983): 2-4, 9.

255. Brenner, George D. "Are Pension Assets Reachable by Creditors?" Journal of the American Society of CLU & ChFC 42 (May 1988): 68-71.

256. Brostoff, Steven. "ERISA Enforcement Targets Servicers." National Underwriter (Life/Health/Financial Services) 90 (December 29, 1986): 3, 16.

257. Brown, M. V. "Prudence Under ERISA: What the Regulators Say." Financial Analysts Journal 33 (January 1977): 33-39.

258. Byland, Terry. "How ERISA Has Affected US Pension Funds." Banker 133 (August 1983): 47-49.

259. Cerino, Ronald J. "Fiduciary Responsibility: Clarifying ERISA's Impact." Pension World 11 (September 1975): 63-86.

260. Chadwick, William J. Regulation of Employee Benefits Brookfield, WI: International Foundation of Employee

Benefit Plans, 1978. 315p.
This work summarizes ERISA and IRS code sections
which pertain to pension and welfare plans. Ap-
plicable labor, securities, equal employment, and
banking laws are also reviewed. Includes a chapter
which briefly describes the functions of those
federal departments and agencies responsible for
the regulation of pension plans.

261. Clay, William L. "The Single Employer Pension Plan
Amendments Act." Labor Law Journal 34 (November
1983): 675-682.

262. Collins, Adrian A. "Pension Regulation; A Study of
Need and Feasibility." DBA dissertation, George Washington University, 1967. 300p.

263. Cooke, James A. "ERISA: No Exit." Traffic Management 22 (May 1983): 53-59.

264. Cooper, William D. "The Multiemployer Pension Plan
Amendments Act of 1980: An Overview." Journal of
Pension Planning & Compliance 12 (Spring 1986): 17-24.

265. Crichton, J. H. "ERISA to ESOP to Capital." Pension
World (June 1978): 58-60+.

266. Dankner, H., and Meyerson, M. "Reporting for ERISA:
A Call for Action Now." Financial Executive 44 (February 1976): 10-12+.

267. Davey, P. J., and Meyer, M. "More Regulation for
Pension Funds?" Conference Board Record 9 (July
1972): 13-18.

268. Dent, J. H. "Inside View of Pension Plan Reform."
Labor Law Journal 24 (November 1973): 715-717.

269. Doyle, James M., Jr. and Green, Richard M. "When
Do Securities Laws Affect Benefit Plans?" Pension
World 24 (May 1988): 44-47.

270. Dunkle, David S. Guide to Pension and Profit Sharing
Plans: Taxation, Selection, and Design. Colorado
Springs, CO: Shepard's/McGraw-Hill, 1984- . (Annual).

A one-volume loose-leaf service which covers current
pension legislation, taxation of pension distributions,
vesting rules, and the regulatory requirements
governing the integration of social security payments
with pension benefits. Pension plan selection and
design, matching pension plans with employers, and
new legal requirements for top heavy plans are other
areas discussed in some detail. Authoritative com-
mentary on structuring a pension or profit-sharing
plan is also included.

271. "ERISA Compliance: A Survey." Institutional Investor
11 (February 1977): 67+.

272. ERISA, the Multiemployer Pension Plan Amendments Act
of 1980. New York: Practising Law Institute, 1984.

273. "ERISA Problems Aired at Pension Forum Hearing /
ERISA Was Worth the Effort but Benefits Now Under
Siege." Employee Benefit Plan Review 39 (January
1985): 77-80.

274. ERISA Qualified Plan Guide. Denver, CO: Pension Pub-
lications of Denver, 1975- . (Bimonthly).
An annotated three-volume (loose-leaf) compendium
of Employee Retirement Income Security Act (ERISA)
requirements for pension and benefit plans. Current
litigation, Treasury Regulations, and those private
and published IRS rulings which effect pension and
benefit plans are annotated and summarized in the
Guide's supplements. Current developments and com-
mentary sections highlight and explain important
pieces of relevant legislation and critical court
rulings.

275. ERISA Update. Washington, DC: Washington Service
Bureau, Inc. (Monthly).
This work provides the latest interpretations and
applications of the Employee Retirement Income
Security Act from the Department of Labor and the
Pension Benefit Guaranty Corporation. Full-text
accounts and abstracts of all opinions are included.

276. Erlenborn, John N. "Was ERISA Worth the Effort?"
Pension World 20 (September 1984): 36-41.

277. "Excess Pension Plan Assets: Whose Money Is It?"
     Employee Benefit Plan Review 40 (October 1985): 15-16.

278. Fannin, R. A. "Don't Let ERISA Stifle Creativity,
     Consultant Says." Business Insurance 11 (November
     28, 1977): 12-25.

279. Ferguson, Dennis H. "The Economic Impact of the
     Employee Retirement Income Security Act on Firms with
     Active and Terminated Pension Plans." Ph.D. disserta-
     tion, Cornell University, 1981. 165p.

280. Fleischer, A., Jr. "Shedding New Light on ERISA."
     Institutional Investor 11 (April 1977): 15+.

281. Fleming, S. "Getting Your Money's Worth from ERISA."
     Personnel 52 (May 1975): 32-43.

282. Frumkin, R., and Schmitt, D. "Pension Improvements
     Since 1974 Reflect Inflation, New US Law." Monthly
     Labor Review 102 (April 1979): 32-37.

283. Geisel, J. "Charting US Pension Policy." Business
     Insurance 13 (July 23, 1979): 1+.

284. Gerstell, Glenn S., and Mackiewicz, Edward R. Pension
     and Welfare Benefits in Bankruptcy. A Course Handbook.
     New York: Practising Law Institute, 1988. 453p.
     The impact of ERISA on benefits, multiemployer
     benefit, and ERISA pension fund claims; the waiver
     of minimum funding standards; and the extension
     of amortization periods are among the topics explored
     in this substantive work.

285. Gertner, Marc. "Attitudes and Approaches of Trustees
     Toward MPPAA." Journal of Pension Planning & Com-
     pliance 9 (April 1983): 159-168.

286. Gill, Kathleen D., ed. ERISA: The Law and The Code.
     Washington, DC: Bureau of National Affairs, 1985.
     325p.

287. Gold, Peter A. "Plan Loans Would Be Restricted Under
     Proposed Regulations." Journal of Compensations &
     Benefits 3 (May/June 1988): 328-335.

288. Goldberg, Seymour. Pension Disputes and Settlements.
      Greenvale, NY: Panel Publishers, 1978.
      A well-organized loose-leaf summary of employee
      benefit plans which is designed to help administrators
      and professional advisors avoid legal, regulatory,
      and internal disputes. Fiduciary liability, reporting
      and disclosure to beneficiaries, civil litigation under
      ERISA, and the internal resolution of disputes are
      among the important areas covered. Tables of cases
      and subject contents are provided for each chapter.

289. Hagigi, Moshe. "Investment Objectives and Policies of
      Large Corporate Pension Funds: Implications for Invest-
      ment and Accounting Regulations." Ph.D. dissertation,
      New York University, 1981. 95p.

290. Hannan, W. F. "More Than Just Fiduciary Problems
      in ERISA." National Underwriter Life and Health In-
      surance Edition 80 (February 7, 1976): 11+.

291. Harris, Anthony A., and Gill, Kathleen D., eds. ERISA:
      The Law and the Code. Washington, DC: Bureau of
      National Affairs, 1987. 389p.
      A full-text compendium of the Employment Retire-
      ment Income Security Act of 1974 as amended in 1986.
      Pertinent sections of the recently amended Internal
      Revenue Code are also included. Editor's notes appear
      at the end of each subsection of the law.

292. Hass, Lawrence J., and Saxon, Stephen M. "Regulation
      of Securities Lending by Pension Plans." Pension World
      19 (May 1983): 26-28.

293. Hawkins, Ralph L., Jr. and Birmingham, Richard J.
      "The Retirement Equity Act of 1984." Journal of Pension
      Planning & Compliance 10 (August 1984): 257-266.

294. Hawthorne, Fran. "How Bob Monks Plans to Shake Up
      Pensionland." Institutional Investor 18 (March 1984):
      112-116, 119.

295. Henle, P., and Schmitt, R. "Pension Reform: The
      Long, Hard Road to Enactment." Monthly Labor Review
      97 (November 1974): 3-12.

296. Hewitt Associates. "Virtually All Pension Plans are
      Affected by New Rules." Personnel Journal 64 (March
      1985): 82-87.

297. Hillman, R. W. "Getting a Determination Letter Under
      ERISA." Practical Accountant 12 (March 1979): 19-23.

298. Hira, Labh S. "Qualified Plans Need Revision to Comply
      with the REA." Tax Adviser 16 (November 1985):
      670-679.

299. Hochheiser, Myron, and Murphy, Richard C. "What
      Does SEPPAA Say About Plan Terminations?" Pension
      World 22 (October 1986): 40-45.

300. Hodges, Leo C. "The Daniel Decision: Its Impact."
      Pension World 15 (March 1979): 20-24.

301. Hollman, Kenneth W., and Murrey, Joe H., Jr. "The
      Basics of Pension Planning." Texas Business Review 57
      (July/August 1983): 181-187.

302. Holmes, W. H. "Proposed Legislation HR 12272." Trusts
      & Estates 112 (June 1973): 446-447+.

303. Hutchinson, J. D. "Ex-pension Chief Eyes the Prudent
      Man Rule Under ERISA." National Underwriter Life and
      Health Insurance Edition 80 (October 9, 1976): 12-15+.

304. Ifflander, A. James, et al. "Western States' Pension
      Plans: Do They Need Federal Regulation?" State Govern-
      ment 58 (Spring 1985): 14-19.

305. Introduction to Qualified Pension and Profit-Sharing Plans.
      New York: Practising Law Institute, 1987. 688p.
          This compendium of legal and regulatory information
      summarizes the Employee Retirement Income Security
      Act of 1974, pension-related court cases, and the
      leading formula contribution plans. Reporting and
      disclosure requirements for pension funds, IRS
      schedules, and an introductory overview of employee
      stock ownership plans (ESOPs) are provided.

306. James, R. M. "ERISA's Heavy Hand Reshapes Pensions."
      Business Insurance 13 (August 20, 1979): 30-31.

307. Kakacek, K. "ERISA: A Risk Management Approach to Fiduciary and Investment Responsibility." Compensation Review 8 (1976): 53-63.

308. Kannel, C. "Urgent ERISA Problems--The Service-Provider/Party in Interest." Trusts & Estates 116 (April 1977): 222-224+.

309. Katz, E. C. "ERISA's Benefit Limitations Un-limited." Pension World 13 (April 1977): 47-50+.

310. Kilberg, William J. "Happy Birthday, ERISA: A Rumination on Recent Developments in ERISA's Exclusive Benefit Rule." Employee Relations Law Journal 10 (Winter 1984/1985): 369-373.

311. Klimkowsky, Beverly M. "Evaluating ERISA." Employee Benefits Journal 7 (December 1982): 25-31.

312. Knox, Peter L. "Minimum Contributions and Benefits in Top-Heavy Plans Clarified by New Proposed Regulations." Taxation for Accountants 31 (September 1983): 134-140.

313. Landsman, Wayne R. "An Investigation of Pension Fund Property Rights." Ph.D. dissertation, Stanford University, 1984. 188p.

314. Langetieg, T. C., et al. "Multiperiod Pension Plans and ERISA Discussion." Journal of Financial & Quantitative Analysis 17 (November 1982): 603-635.

315. Lanoff, I[an] D. "Reporting and Disclosure and Prudence in Investment Under ERISA." Labor Law Journal 29 (June 1978): 323-329.

316. Lanoff, Ian D. "The Social Investment of Private Pension Plan Assets: May It Be Done Lawfully Under ERISA?" Labor Law Journal 31 (July 1980): 387-392.

317. Leaton, Edward K. "Comments on TEFRA's Pension Provisions." CPA Journal 53 (March 1983): 40-48.

318. Lindquist, J. R. "Pension Remodeling Act of 1974." Taxes 52 (December 1974): 873-880.

319. LoCicero, J. A. "How to Cope with the Multi-Employer
      Pension Plan Amendments Act of 1980." Personnel Ad-
      ministration 26 (May 1981): 51-54+.

320. Luris, Alvin D. "Reforming ERISA: Ten Pension Com-
      mandments." Journal of Pension Planning & Compliance
      10 (December 1984): 405-409.

321. Malley, Susan L. "Unfunded Pension Liabilities and the
      Cost of Equity Capital." Financial Review 18 (May 1983):
      133-145.

322. Mamorsky, Jeffrey D. "New Regulations Issued on Top-
      Heavy Plans." Corporation Law Review 6 (Fall 1983):
      374-380.

323. Mamorsky, J[effrey] D., and Wolf, C. B. "Identifying
      the ERISA Fiduciary." Pension World 14 (June 1978):
      46-48+.

324. "A Mandate on Benefits: There's Legislation to Guide
      Pension Management." Pensions & Investment Age.
      Pensions Management Mid-American Supplement (Spring
      1987): 37-38.

325. Maynard, Philip, and Anthony, F. Lee. "Bridging the
      TEFRA Pension Gap." United States Banker 96 (January
      1985): 47-50.

326. McCord, Thomas, and Doreian, Raymond. ERISA Plan
      Administrator's Desk Book with Checklists and Guidelines
      for Successful Communications. 2nd ed. Englewood
      Cliffs, NJ: Institute for Business Planning, 1979.
      392p.
          A basic guide designed to assist pension administrators
      in meeting federal reporting requirements and time-
      tables as stipulated in the Employee Retirement Income
      Security Act of 1974. The development of annual
      reports, plan descriptions, and communication programs
      for pension and deferred income plans are presented.
      Includes samples of federal reporting forms and em-
      ployee benefit applications.

327. McKee, J. W., and Hindenach, L. P. "Corporation and
      ERISA: For Now and for the Future." Financial Execu-
      tive 43 (June 1975): 16-22.

328. McManus, G. J. "Is Industry Ready to Go on New
Pension Act?" Iron Age 216 (December 1, 1975): 25-27.

329. McMillan, Henry M. "Nonassignable Pensions and the
Price of Risk." Journal of Money, Credit & Banking
18 (February 1986): 60-75.

330. Melbinger, Michael S. "Narrowing the Protection of
Pension Benefits in Bankruptcy Proceedings." Employee
Relations Law Journal 12 (Winter 1986/1987): 397-411.

331. "Minimum Funding Standards and Limitations Are Nar-
rowed by 1987 Budget Reconciliation Act." Employee
Benefit Plan Review 42 (April 1988): 48-52.

332. Misher, Norman J. "Recent Developments in Employee
Benefits: Revenue Rulings on Pension and Profit-Sharing
Plans." Journal of Pension Planning & Compliance 11
(Fall 1985): 251-257.

333. Mueller, R. J. "What Practitioners Should Know About
the Expanded Role of the Actuary Under ERISA."
Journal of Taxation 42 (March 1975): 149-153.

334. Mulholland, J. "Hearings Begin on Move to Simplify
ERISA." National Underwriter Life and Health Insurance
Edition 83 (December 8, 1979): 4-5+.

335. Myers, R. J. "New Social Security Amendments: How
They Affect Private Pension Plans." Pension World 14
(March 1978): 14-18.

336. Olsen, Bradley A., and Woolever, Michael H. "Managing
Pension Fund Properties: The Prohibited Transaction
Rules of ERISA." Journal of Property Management 48
(May/June 1983): 7-9, 54-55.

337. Osgood, Russell K. The Law of Pensions and Profit-
Sharing: Qualified Retirement Plans and Other Deferred
Compensation Arrangements. Boston: Little, Brown
& Co., 1984. 454p.
   An excellent overview and explanation of each statu-
   tory provision pertaining to pension plans. Relevant
   treasury regulations, revenue rulings, tax court mem-
   orandum, and court cases are explicated. Includes
   tables of court cases and Internal Revenue Code sections.

338.   Overbeck, J. H., Jr. "Persons Upon Whom Duties
        and Obligations Are Imposed Under the Employee Retire-
        ment Income Security Act of 1974." Taxes 52 (December
        1974): 881-895.

339.   Pensions, Profit-Sharing, and Other Deferred Compensa-
        tion Plans. Philadelphia: American Law Institute-
        American Bar Association Committee on Continuing Pro-
        fessional Education, 1982. 551p.
        A collection of lectures delivered by pension plan
        experts during a 1982 course of study and program
        in San Francisco. Age discrimination in employee
        benefit plans, actuarial techniques and options for
        pension cost acceleration, plan disqualification--effects
        and alternative actions, and pension plan loans to
        participants are among the topics explored.

340.   Pension Reform Act of 1974. Chicago: Commerce Clear-
        ing House, 1974.

341.   "Pension Reform's Expensive Ricochet." Business Week
        (March 24, 1975): 144-150+.

342.   "Pension Reversions: Who Owns the $100 Billion?"
        Regulation 8 (March/April 1984): 11-12, 40.

343.   "Pension Vesting and the IRS: The Power of Regulatory
        Persistence." Regulation 7 (November/December 1983):
        9-12.

344.   Pensions and Deferred Compensation. Chicago: Com-
        merce Clearing House, 1988- . (Monthly).
        A nontechnical guide which explains government rules
        applying to a variety of retirement benefit and pension
        plans. Retirement planning strategies, plan termina-
        tion, plan qualification requirements, and fiduciary
        responsibility are among the key areas regularly
        covered. A newsletter highlighting the contents of
        the current reports section is also provided.

345.   Petrovsky, Seymour. "Despite TEFRA, Pensions Won't
        Die." Life Association News 79 (May 1984): 134-143.

346.   Plutchok, Jonathan. "Back into the Blender." Financial
        Planning 13 (September 1984): 227-230.

347. Plutchok, Jonathan. "Lump Sums, PT Rules and Pension Raids." Financial Planning 13 (May 1984): 151-154.

348. Posnick, Mark K., and Johnson, Douglas E. "Doing Business with the Pension Funds." Mortgage Banking 43 (November 1982): 39-43.

349. Power, Christopher. "The Best-Laid Plans." Forbes 135 (January 28, 1985): 86-87.

350. Pritzker, Malcolm L. "Arbitration of Employer Withdrawal Liability." Employee Benefits Journal 7 (December 1982): 22-24, 31.

351. "Recent Changes to Qualified Plans Amplified in Temporary Regulations." Taxation for Accountants 36 (April 1986): 210-211.

352. Reichler, R. "Expanded Labor Reporting Requirements Under the New Pension Reform Legislation." Journal of Taxation 41 (December 1974): 333-335+.

353. "Retirement: For Many, a Dream Gone up in Smoke." Office 95 (February 1982): 31, 34.

354. Rizzo, R. S. "Plural Employee Plans Under ERISA: Withdrawals by Contributing Employers and Plan Terminations." Trusts & Estates 114 (September 1975): 602-604+.

355. Salisbury, Dallas [L.] "Washington: The Benefit Planner's Nightmare." FE: The Magazine for Financial Executives 3 (March 1987): 8-18.

356. Salisbury, Dallas L., et al. "ERISA's 10th Anniversary." Business Insurance 18 (August 27, 1984): 25-27.

357. Schreitmueller, R. G. "Living with ERISA Administration." Personnel Administrator 22 (May 1977): 26-31+.

358. "Senator Harrison A. Williams on ERISA." Pension World 13 (May 1977): 35-38.

359. Sarnick, Wayne R. "Retroactive Pension Legislation: Pension Benefit Guaranty Corp. V. R. A. Gray & Co." Tax Lawyer 38 (Winter 1985): 491-497.

360. Sheean, J. B. "To Comply with ERISA, Investment
      Philosophies May Be?" Pension World 13 (March 1977):
      18-20.

361. Sheil, D. R. "Determining the Right of Pension Claimants:
      Before and After ERISA." Labor Law Journal 30 (Feb-
      ruary 1979): 88-101.

362. Simone, Joseph R., and Riemer, Scott M. "Discretionary
      or Conditional Forms of Benefit Distribution Under Pro-
      posed Regulations." Journal of Pension Planning &
      Compliance 12 (Fall 1986): 211-220.

363. Sirkin, Michael S., and Sirkin, Stuart A. "The Effect
      of the TEFRA Pension Provisions on Closely Held and
      Professional Businesses." Review of Taxation of Indi-
      viduals 7 (Spring 1983): 99-122.

364. Skolnik, A. M. "Pension Reform Legislation of 1974."
      Social Security Bulletin 37 (December 1974): 35-42.

365. Smith, Lowell C. "An Evaluation of Public Policy Pro-
      posals for the Regulation of Private Pension Plan Eligi-
      bility Requirements and Vesting Provisions." Ph.D.
      dissertation, University of Alabama, 1969. 380p.

366. Stein, Paul C., and Schier, Lewis. "How the New Tax
      Law Affects Pension Plans." Journal of Pension Planning
      & Compliance 10 (August 1984): 245-256.

367. Stone, Mary S.; Frecka, Thomas J.; and Jamison,
      Robert W. "Multiemployer Pension Plan Amendments
      Act." CPA Journal 51 (December 1981): 34-37, 40.

368. Stuchinew, T. B. "Working with the New, Tougher
      Funding Requirements of the Pension Reform Law."
      Journal of Taxation 41 (November 1974): 272-276.

369. "Study: ERISA Falling Short of Its Intention." Pensions
      & Investment Age 14 (September 29, 1986): 8, 73.

370. Sturgess, Tom, and Schwartz, Richard. "The Multi-
      employer Pension Plan Amendments Act of 1980--Let the
      Buyer Beware." Journal of Buyouts & Acquisitions 1
      (February 1983): 2-7.

371. Thompson, A. Frank, et al. "Pension Liability Reporting
     Under ERISA." Employee Benefits Journal 8 (March
     1983): 2-7, 27.

372. Tolley, H. Dennis, and Randall, Boyd C. "A Statistical
     Test for Discrimination in Coverage in Employee Benefit
     Plans." Journal of Pension Planning & Compliance 12
     (Spring 1986): 37-49.

373. Tracy, Thomas G., and Moore, Kim. "The Top-Heavy
     Pension Plan Rules Under TEFRA: Parity for Some,
     Disparity for Others." Tax Adviser 14 (September 1983):
     514-524.

374. Treynor, Jack L. The Financial Reality of Pension
     Funding Under ERISA. Homewood, IL: Dow Jones-
     Irwin, 1976. 149p.
         An excellent examination of ERISA's impact on pension
     planning. The implications of ERISA on the Pension
     Benefit Guaranty Corporation are outlined. Includes
     a glossary of terms and appendices of actuarial cost
     methods, and the major provisions of ERISA.

375. United States. Congress. Conference Committees, 1974.
     Employee Retirment Income Security Act 1974. Washing-
     ton, DC: U. S. Govt. Print Office, 1974.

376. United States. Congress. House. Committee on Edu-
     cation and Labor. Subcommittee on Labor Standards.
     Oversight on the Employee Retirement Income Security
     Act of 1974. Washington, DC: U.S. Govt. Print.
     Office, 1975.

377. United States. Congress. House. Committee on Edu-
     cation and Labor. Subcommittee on Labor Standards.
     Oversight on ERISA, 1978. Washington, DC: U.S.
     Govt. Print. Office, 1978.

378. United States. Congress. House. Committee on Small
     Business. Subcommittee on SBA and SBIC Authority
     and General Small Business Problems. ERISA's Impact
     on Small Business. Washington, DC: U.S. Govt. Print.
     Office, 1978.
         A full-text report of the House Subcommittee hearings
     of October 11 and 14, 1977, on the effects of ERISA

on pension plans offered by small business. Termination statistics from the Government Accounting Office and the PBGC are included in the report's appendices. The results of a questionnaire on the causes of pension plan terminations and pension plan characteristics are also provided.

379. United States. Congress. House. Committee on Ways and Means. Subcommittee on Oversight. Employee Retirement Income Security Act of 1974. Washington, DC: U.S. Govt. Print. Office, 1976.

380. United States. Congress. House. Committee on Ways and Means. Subcommittee on Oversight. Pension Reform Act of 1974. Washington, DC: U.S. Govt. Print. Office, 1975.

381. United States. Congress. Senate. Committee on Finance. Subcommittee on Private Pension Plans and Employee Fringe Benefits. Pension Simplification and Investment Rules. Washington, DC: U.S. Govt. Print. Office, 1977.

382. United States. Congress. Senate. Committee on Human Resources. Subcommittee on Labor. ERISA Improvements Act of 1978. Washington, DC: U.S. Govt. Print. Office, 1978.

383. "Virtually All Pension Plans Are Affected by the New Rules." Personnel Journal 64 (March 1985): 82-86.

384. Walker, Deborah, and Goldstein, Robert E. "How to Relieve Pension Tension." Management Focus 31 (July/ August 1984): 30-35.

385. Webster, George D. "Retirement Equity Act Protects Women's Pension Rights." Association Management 36 (November 1984): 45-51.

386. Werner, Charles A., and Kostolansky, John W. "Accounting Liabilities Under the Multiemployer Pension Plan Amendments Act." Journal of Accounting, Auditing & Finance 7 (Spring 1984): 212-224.

387. Wilf, M. M. "Limitations on Benefits and Contributions

for Corporate Employees Under New Pension Law."
Journal of Taxation 41 (November 1974): 280-286.

388. Wilkie, Robert C., and Holbrook, Martin E. Pension
Reform Handbook: Employee Retirement Income Security
Act of 1974 (ERISA) and Later Amendments. Englewood,
NJ: Prentice-Hall, 1987.

389. "Williams-Javits Bill Seen Benefiting From Rival's Com-
plexity." National Underwriter Life & Health Insurance
Edition 77 (September 8, 1973): 1+.

390. Wray, A. Victor, and Silverman, Pamela K. "Qualified
Plans Will Again Require Revision After the Retirement
Equity Act of 1984." Journal of Taxation 62 (January
1985): 12-18.

MANAGEMENT/ADMINISTRATION

391. Alden, Philip M., Jr. "Are You Spending Too Much on Pensions?" Pension World 21 (May 1985): 54-57.

392. Allen, Everett T. Pension Planning. 4th ed. Homewood, IL: R. D. Irwin, 1981. 423p.
Intended for college students, this textbook covers many of the important aspects of pension fund management and administration. Among the topics examined are private pension plans, trust fund plans, the taxation of distributions, disclosure requirements, and the Employee Retirement Income Security Act of 1974. Includes numerous explanatory references.

393. Ambachtsheer, Keith P. Pension Funds and the Bottom Line; Managing the Corporate Pension Fund as a Financial Business. Homewood, IL: Dow Jones-Irwin, 1986. 167p.
This work explores the fundamental principles and practices currently associated with pension fund investment and management. Investment strategy and structure, policy implementation, control systems, and the legitimacy of private pensions are among the topics covered. Explanatory references are included for each chapter.

394. An Analysis of Pension Plan Costs, 1972-1976; Final Report, 1980. Washington, DC: U.S. Department of Labor, 1980. 113p.
An analytical study of the major factors affecting private pension costs. Estimates of trends in pension plan contributions, a review of the potential impact of the major factors on contribution trends, and the provision of specific analytical tools for the Office of Pension and Welfare Benefit Programs were the primary objectives of the project. Appendices include statistical data from the Department of Labor.

395. Arnott, Robert D. "The Pension Sponsor's View of
      Asset Allocation." Financial Analysts Journal 41
      (September/October 1985): 17-23.

396. Bicksler, James L., et al. "The Integration of Insurance
      and Taxes in Corporate Pension Strategy/Discussion."
      Journal of Finance 40 (July 1985): 943-957.

397. Bodie, Zvi, et al. "Corporate Pension Policy: An
      Empirical Investigation." Financial Analysts Journal
      41 (September/October 1985): 10-16.

398. Bret, William N., Jr. "The Actuary's New Assumptions."
      Pension World 11 (November 1975): 31-66.

399. Bronson, Dorrance C. Concepts of Actuarial Soundness
      in Pension Plans. Homewood, IL: R. D. Irwin, 1957.
      183p.
      An analysis of the acturial principles and practices
      associated with the administration of pensions. Key
      areas considered include funding methods, reserve
      assets and liabilities, actuarial assumptions, and
      governmental regulation. Footnoted references and
      tabular charts are provided.

400. Buppert, W. I. "What the Supervisor Should Know About
      ERISA." Supervisory Management 20 (August 1975):
      11-14.

401. Burianek, F. G. "Using Financial Ratios to Analyze
      Pension Liabilities." Financial Executive 49 (January
      1981): 29-36.

402. Burr, Barry B. "Who Controls Pension Surplus?"
      Latest Ruling Upholds Carbide's Use of a 'Parachute'."
      Pensions & Investment Age 14 (February 17, 1986):
      34.

403. Clark, Robert Louis. Cost-Effective Pension Planning.
      New York: Pergamon Press, 1982. 38p.
      A brief summary of the key areas associated with
      pension fund management including labor turnover,
      age structure of the labor force, increased net
      compensation, inflation, and employee development and
      training. A suggested readings list, abstracts of

articles and books, and statistical information are
provided.

404.   Cleary, William T., Jr. "Don't Tempt a Corporate Take-
        over Through an Overfunded Pension Plan." Management
        Review 76 (June 1987): 51-52.

405.   Connors, J. A. "How to Handle Pension Liabilities in
        Corporate Acquisitions." Pension World 13 (January
        1977): 44-48.

406.   Cooper, Robert D. Pension Fund Operations and Ex-
        penses. Brookfield, WI: International Foundation of
        Employee Benefit Plans, 1984. 102p.
            This empirical study examines collectively bargained,
        multiemployer, defined benefit plans. A description
        of fund operations, statistical data, and variables
        affecting the study are clearly presented. Includes
        explanatory references and supporting tables and
        figures.

407.   Costa, Michael L. Master Trust: Simplifying Employee
        Benefits Trust Fund Administration. New York:
        Amacom, 1980. 213p.
            A helpful guide which examines the operation and
        management of pension and benefit trust fund manage-
        ment. Fiduciary responsibility, establishing and im-
        plementing investment objectives, the selection of a
        master trustee, and monitoring investment performance
        are among the key areas covered.

408.   Covaleski, John. "Pension Funds Face Negative Cash
        Flow." Pensions & Investment Age 15 (July 1987): 2,
        39.

409.   Crawford, Diane. "Computer Power Boosts Pension As-
        set Management at Olin Corp." Wall Street Computer
        Review 2 (April 1985): 9-12.

410.   Crowell, R. A., and Mainer, R. E. "Pension Fund
        Management: External or Internal?" Harvard Business
        Review 58 (November/December 1980): 180-182.

411.   Dase, J. "Pension Fund Management: A New Do-It-
        Yourself Approach." Pension World 14 (April 1978):
        12-14+.

412. Davey, Patrick J. Financial Management of Company
Pension Plans. New York: Conference Board, 1973.
117p.
A timely study which provides basic information about
the financial management of trusteed pension plans.
Plan design, benefit financing, pension fund asset
investment, the evaluation of investment performance,
and current and pending legislation are key areas
examined. A selected bibliography and statistical
tables are included.

413. Doyle, A. M., Jr. "Pension Fund Assets: Help for
the Small Corporation?" Financial Executive 43 (August
1975): 28-31.

414. Ellis, C. D. "Pension Funds Need Management Management." Financial Analysts Journal 35 (May 1979): 25-
28.

415. Fenske, Doris. "Shifting the Actuarial Burden."
Best's Review Life and Health Insurance Edition 84
(May 1983): 12-16.

416. Feuer, Philip J. "Get Senior Management Involved in
the Pension Plan." Financial Executive 50 (November
1982): 24-26, 28-30.

417. Figgie, Harry E., Jr. "Defusing the Pension Liability
Bomb." Harvard Business Review 59 (November/
December 1981): 157-163.

418. Finn, E. "Case for Co-Management of Employee Pension
Funds." Labour Gazette 73 (June 1973): 356-365.

419. Fisher, M. J. "Senator Raps Pension Fund Management."
National Underwriter Life and Health Insurance Edition
82 (October 7, 1978): 2+.

420. Frankel, Tamar. "Board Liability for Pension Plans."
Directors & Boards 10 (Summer 1986): 26-27.

421. Gardner, Esmond B., ed. Pension Fund Investment
Management. Homewood, IL: R. D. Irwin, 1969. 141p.
A general overview of the funding, investment practice, and ethics of pension trusts. A selected bibliography is provided.

422. Goldberg, Seymour. "Pension Planning and the CPA."
      Journal of Accountancy 157 (May 1984):   68-72.

423. Gray, Hillel. New Directions in the Investment and
      Control of Pension Funds. Washington, DC: Investor
      Responsibility Research Center, 1983.   120p.
      This excellent book briefly traces the development
      of pension funds and the importance of their growth
      over the last 100 years. The issue of state govern-
      ment and union control of pension investment, an
      analysis of the statutes regulating alternative fund
      investment, are also presented. Includes a short
      list of sources used in the report's preparation.

424. "Greenmailers Beware: Pension Funds Are on the Prowl."
      Journal of Buyouts & Acquisitions 3 (June/July 1985):
      9-13.

425. Gropper, Diane H. "How to Switch Managers Without
      Losing Your Shirt." Institutional Investor 18 (July
      1984):   115-120.

426. Gropper, Diane H. "Pension Management: What Do
      You Say After You Say You're Sorry?" Institutional
      Investor 18 (December 1984):   115-121.

427. Gropper, Diane H. "Pensions: The View from the
      Top." Institutional Investor 17 (March 1983):   85-95.

428. Haake, A. P., Jr. "Pension Fund Patterns; Their
      Management and Growth Plans." Financial Executive
      33 (April 1965):   37-38+.

429. Haneberg, Ronald L. "Pension Forecasting--A Valuable
      Planning Tool." Pension World 18 (November 1982):
      36-40.

430. Harkins, E. P., and Thompson, G. C. "Administering
      and Evaluating the Investment of Trusteed Pension Plan
      Funds." Conference Board Record 2 (December 1965):
      24-30.

431. Hayes, William. "In-House Pension Fund Management:
      A Viable Alternative?" Pension World 14 (November
      1978):   26-28.

432. Heard, James E. "Pension Funds and Contests for Corporate Control." California Management Review 29 (Winter 1987): 89-100.

433. Hemmerick, Steve. "Executives' Effect Measured." Pensions & Investment Age 15 (May 4, 1987): 3, 44.

434. Hesmondhalgh, S. "Union Participation in Pension Fund Management." Personnel Management 9 (September 1977): 24-28.

435. Hieb, Elizabeth A., ed. Proceedings of the 1977 Institute on Employer Contributions, Collections and Control, Payroll Auditing, November 27-30, 1977, Hollywood, Florida. Brookfield, WI: International Foundation of Employee Benefit Plans, 1977. 163p.
   This work includes edited accounts of the presentations of pension administrators, union officials, and legal experts delivered during the conference. The impact of the collective bargaining agreement on collection procedures, accounting and auditing guidelines for delinquency audits, enforcement through legal procedures, and alternative collection methods for delinquent accounts are among the topics addressed. An appendix of relevant legal cases is provided.

436. "How Firms are Shaping Their Retirement Plans." Management Methods 15 (January 1959): 36-40.

437. "How to Run a Profitable Pension Fund." Commercial and Financial Chronicle 217 (February 15, 1973): 625+.

438. Ippolito, Richard A. "The Economic Burden of Corporate Pension Liabilities." Financial Analysts Journal 42 (January/February 1986): 22-34.

439. Jansson, Solveig. "Pension Management: How a Down-Home Manner Pays Off for Duff & Phelps." Institutional Investor 21 (January 1987): 159-160.

440. Jost, Lee F. Guide to Professional Benefit Plan Management and Administration. Brookfield, WI: International Foundation of Employee Benefit Plans, 1980. 405p.
   A manual, intended for practitioners, which provides extensive coverage of the history and current practice

of joint labor-management employee benefit trust
fund administration. The role of the professional
administrative manager, decision making and policy
execution, accounting and record maintenance, and
notification requirements to plan participants and
beneficiaries are topics featured. Includes appendices
of the compliance enforcement procedural manual,
an annual actuarial report, section 302 of the Labor-
Management Relations Act of 1947, and Department of
Labor auditing guidelines for Welfare and Pension
Benefit Plans.

441. Kent, Glenn H. "Team Management of Pension Money."
      Harvard Business Review 57 (May/June 1979): 162-167.

442. Knowles, Bob. "Employers Eye Pension Costs." National
      Underwriter (Property/Casualty/Employee Benefits) 91
      (January 26, 1987): 19, 30.

443. Kraabel, Stephen E. "Hidden Pension Costs." Benefits
      Quarterly 1 (Fourth Quarter 1985): 34-40.

444. Krauss, Alan. "Pensions Shareholders Exercising Proxy
      Vote." Pensions & Investment Age 14 (March 31, 1986):
      1, 52-53.

445. Lang, Larry. "Why Does Our Pension Plan Cost So
      Much?" Pension World 21 (April 1985): 44-47.

446. Logue, Dennis E. Managing Corporate Pension Plans:
      The Impacts of Inflation. Washington, DC: American
      Enterprise Institute for Public Policy Research 1984.
      68p.
      A brief study which examines the effects of inflation
      on the pension system in the private sector. A case
      study analysis of one company's pension fund is
      presented to illustrate the influence of investment
      decision making on benefit levels. Footnoted referen-
      ces and statistical tables are included.

447. Lohrer, Richard B. "An Open Road to Master Trusts."
      Pension World 13 (September 1977): 11-14.

448. Madden, William B. "The New Focus on Managing
      Pension Plans." Financial Executive 52 (April 1984):
      15-18.

449. Mainer, Robert. "How to Manage Your Pension Fund
     Management." Financial Executive 4 (January/February
     1988): 22-27.

450. Maldonado, K. F. "Elapsed Time Method for Crediting
     Service Can Reduce Plan Administrative Expenses."
     Journal of Taxation 54 (February 1981): 84-88.

451. Malecki, Donald S. "Insuring the Employee Benefits
     Program: A Tale of Two Policies." Rough Notes 130
     (February 1987): 30, 32.

452. Mamorsky, Jeffrey D. Pension and Profit Sharing: A
     Basic Guide. New York: Executive Enterprise, 1978.
     301p.
     A book intended to serve as a manual for business-
     men, attorneys, and other professionals responsible
     for pension plan management and administration.
     Plan termination, pension funding, plan participation,
     and reporting and disclosure requirements are ex-
     plained. Includes a chapter on the Internal Revenue
     Service's pension plan qualification procedures.

453. Margady, Myles. "How to Manage Pension Plans in
     Mergers." Harvard Business Review 57 (July/August
     1979): 40-49.

454. Mazzella, Donald P. "Pension Planning Software: How
     Trustees Invest in Your Old Age." Wall Street Computer
     Review 4 (April 1987): 57-62.

455. McGinn, Daniel F. Actuarial Fundamentals for Multi-
     employer Plans. Brookfield, WI: International Foundation
     of Employee Benefit Plans, 1982. 122p.
     A definitive text which explains the role of the
     actuary in establishing the objectives, provisions,
     and requirements of multi-employer pension plans.
     Actuarial cost methods and employer withdrawal lia-
     bilities are also examined. Mortality, job turnover,
     and retirement rate assumption tables are included
     in the works' appendices.

456. McHugh, W. J. "ERISA--A New Audit Headache for
     Management." Management Accounting 57 (April 1976):
     21-28.

457.   Melone, Victor J.   "Money Management--The Large Firm's
       Advantages."   Pension World 18 (November 1982):   42-
       44, 68.

458.   Municipal Finance Officers Association of the United
       States and Canada.   Committee on Public Employee Retire-
       ment Administration.   1976 Retirement Proceedings:
       Papers Presented at the 70th Annual MFOA Conference
       on Public Finance, San Francisco, May 2-6, 1976.
       Chicago: The Association, 1976.   120p.
       A collection of papers which address such pension-
       related issues as ERISA, federal regulation of public
       pensions, pension fund investment strategy, and the
       management of risk in security portfolios.   Financial
       analysts, labor relations specialists, and pension ad-
       ministrators are among those contributing to the pro-
       ceedings.

459.   Niland, Powell.   "Reforming Private Pension Plan Adminis-
       tration."   Business Horizons 19 (February 1976):   25-35.

460.   "The 1988 Pension Olympics."   Institutional Investor
       22 (February 1988):   77-112.

461.   O'Brien, John C.   "An Analysis of the Standards of
       Administration of Union Welfare and Pension Funds."
       Ph.D. dissertation, University of Notre Dame, 1961.
       495p.

462.   Pension Asset Management: The Corporate Decision:
       A Research Study.   New York: FERF, 1980.   285p.
       A report intended for those executives responsible
       for the investment of their corporation's pension funds.
       The determination of investment strategy, measure-
       ment of portfolio performance and return, and the
       selection of external fund managers are several of
       the areas covered.   An excellent chapter on asset
       allocation and the procedures for simulating risk and
       return is also featured.

463.   Pension Plan Forms With Lurie's Commentaries on Pension
       Design.   Jacksonville, FL: Corbel & Co.   (Irregular).

464.   Perham, John C.   "Look for Fireworks at Annual
       Meetings."   Business Month 129 (April 1987):   26-28.

465. Rapoport, Roger. "Jesse Unruh: The Guardian Angel
      on Wall Street." Business & Society Review 56 (Winter
      1986): 26-29.

466. Rohrer, Julie. "Pension Management: Where Has All
      the Marketing Talent Gone?" Institutional Investor 17
      (December 1983): 141-152.

467. Rohrer, Julie. "The Return of the Star System."
      Institutional Investor 17 (May 1983): 89-94, 96.

468. Rudd, Andrew. "Investment Manager Selection."
      Journal of Accounting, Auditing & Finance 7 (Summer
      1984): 393-396.

469. Schonbak, Judith. "Changing Demographics: The
      Effect on Pensions." Pension World 16 (March 1980):
      54-57.

470. Shepherd, A. G., ed. Pension Fund Administration.
      Cambridge: England: ICSA Publishing, 1984. 182p.
      A substantive overview of pension plan management
      by eight leading investment specialists. The ex-
      tablishment of a pension scheme, control of fund in-
      vestments, investment performance, the statutory
      responsibilities of administrators, and company take-
      overs and pension mergers are several of the major
      areas addressed. Includes a glossary of pension
      terms, a guide to statutory references, and appendi-
      ces.

471. Simms, C. R. "Current Pension Problems and Inflation:
      New Changes and Complications Call for More Flexible
      Funding Methods." Controller 28 (April 1960): 157-
      161+.

472. Slimmon, Robert F. Successful Pension Design for Small-
      to-Medium-Sized Businesses. 2nd ed. Englewood Cliffs,
      NJ: Prentice-Hall, 1987. 440p.
      An up-to-date text which explains how to establish
      and implement pension plans. Profit sharing, unit
      benefit, defined contribution, and money purchase
      pensions are among the plans covered. Appendices
      include planning documents and checklists.

473. Stolte, M. D. "Pension Plan Sponsors: Monitor Your-
      selves." Harvard Business Review 59 (March/April
      1981): 136-143.

474. Stout, Donald F. "New Pension Option for High-Level
      Managers." Harvard Business Review 54 (September/
      October 1976): 128-132.

475. Trowbridge, C. L. "ABC's of Pension Funding."
      Harvard Business Review 44 (March 1966): 115-126.

476. Weiss, Marc A. Pension Fund Investments: The Issue
      of Control. Palo Alto, CA: Center for Economic Studies,
      1978. 58p.
      A noteworthy Study which recommends greater
      governmental and community control over the private
      and public investment of pension funds. The re-
      direction of pension fund capital to more socially
      responsible uses and for the direct benefit of em-
      ployees is proposed. Includes a bibliography and
      supporting statistical data.

477. White, Rich. "In Search of DOL's Prudent Man."
      Pension World 15 (November 1979): 38-45.

MATHEMATICAL ANALYSIS

478. Anderson, Arthur W. Pension Mathematics for Actuaries.
      Needham, MD: Arthur W. Anderson, 1985. 175p.
      A technical guide which explores actuarial cost methods
      and the calculation of contributory plans and ancillary
      benefits. Numerous pension benefit and vesting
      formulas, plus explanations, are presented. Includes
      an index to the principal algebraic symbols used in
      the text.

479. Dorsey, Stuart. "A Model and Empirical Estimates of
      Worker Pension Coverage in the U.S." Southern Economic
      Journal 49 (October 1982): 506-520.

480. Fosu, Augustin K. "Impact of Unionism on Pension
      Fringes." Industrial Relations 22 (Fall 1983): 419-425.

481. Ippolito, Richard A. "The Economic Function of Under-
      funded Pension Plans." Journal of Law & Economics
      28 (October 1985): 611-651.

482. Marks, Barry L., and Raman, K. K. "Pension Ratios
      as 'Correlates' of Municipal Pension Underfunding."
      Journal of Accounting & Public Policy 4 (Summer 1985):
      149-157.

483. Schiller, B. R., and Weiss, R. D. "Pensions and Wages:
      A Test for Equalizing Differences." Review of Economics
      and Statistics 62 (November 1980): 529-538.

484. Assessment of Special Rules Exempting Employers Withdrawing from Multiemployer Pension Plans from Withdrawal
Liability. Washington, DC: U.S. General Accounting
Office, 1984. 54p.
This government report analyzes the effect of the
Multiemployer Plan Amendment Act on those firms in
the construction, trucking, and entertainment in-
dustries that have withdrawn from multiemployer
pension plans. Income/benefit, asset/benefit and
expense/benefit ratios are included for each industry
in the report's appendices.

485. Cozort, Larry A. "The Effect of Accrued Pension Benefit Preservation on Worker Mobility in Multi-employer
Plans." Ph.D. dissertation, Virginia Polytechnic Institute and State University, 1985. 129p.

486. Lawler, Kathy A. "Multiemployer Plan Costs on Mass
Terminations Can Be Controlled." Journal of Compensation & Benefits 3 (March/April 1988): 295-298.

487. LoCicero, Joseph A. Multiemployer Pension Plans.
Morristown, NJ: Financial Executives Research Foundation, 1985. 21p.
A brief guide for employers which outlines the basic
financial and legal obligations associated with establishing and maintaining private pension programs.
A summary of the major provisions of the Multiemployer Pension Plan Amendments Act (MPPAA) of
1980 is included in the work's appendix.

488. O'Reilly, Timothy P., and Spencer, Steven H. "Effective
Collection of Multiemployer Withdrawal Liabilities."
Journal of Pension Planning & Compliance 9 (August
1983): 279-290.

489. Walters, Donald A. "Multiemployer Fund Offers More
      Benefits, Same Contributions." Pension World 22 (November 1986): 37-38.

PENSION BENEFIT GUARANTEE CORPORATION

490. Amoroso, Vincent. "PBGC Interest Rates." Employee
      Benefits Journal 11 (September 1986): 22-24, 38.

491. "CBO Publishes Study of PBGC's Financial Condition,
      Congress Enacts Changes in Premium." Employee Benefit
      Plan Review 42 (March 1988): 18-22.

492. "Few Large Underfunded Plans, Many Overfunded Re-
      versions Characterize Current Status of PBGC." Em-
      ployee Benefit Plan Review 40 (December 1985): 69-74.

493. Gropper, Diane H. "How the PBGC Hopes to Fill Its
      Coffers." Institutional Investor 18 (August 1984): 91-93.

494. Hankin, Sam. "Exclusive Interview: Kathleen Utgoff
      Takes Over the PBGC." Pension World 21 (October
      1985): 38-41.

495. Jones, Edwin M. "PBGC at the Crossroads." Labor
      Law Journal 34 (June 1983): 323-331.

496. Jones, Edwin M. "PBGC's Critical Needs." Labor
      Law Journal 33 (November 1982): 699-703.

497. Kutz, Karen S. "Steel Industry Crisis Impacts Entire
      Private Pension System." Pension World 23 (July 1987):
      28-33.

498. Munnell, Alicia H. "Guaranteeing Private Pension
      Benefits: A Potentially Expensive Business." New
      England Economic Review (March/April 1982): 24-47.

499. O'Toole, Patricia, and Zanders, Katharena L. "How
      Safe Is Your Pension?" Fortune 114 (October 27, 1986):
      52-56.

500. "PBGC Battles for Premium Increase." Pension World
      21 (July 1985): 38-40, 57.

501. "PBGC's Stability Dependent on Premium Increases, but
      Reorganization Improves Operational Efficiency." Employee
      Benefit Plan Review 38 (March 1984): 68-71.

502. Smith, Brian P. "Pension Insurance Fund Suffers from
      FSLIC-Like Woes." Savings Institutions 106 (December
      1985): 124-125.

503. Tharp, Charles C. "Legislative Changes Needed for
      PBGC." Labor Law Journal 35 (June 1984): 323-328.

504. Walker, David M. "The PBGC's Role in Protecting
      Lump-Sum Benefit Values." Labor Law Journal 35
      (November 1984): 667-670.

505. Cirino, R. "Pension Officer Vs. the Board." Institutional Investor 11 (March 1977): 297-299.

506. Cottle, Sidney. "How to Hire a Pension Fund Manager." Financial Executive 51 (February 1983): 50-59.

507. Dannen, Fredric. "Pensions: Who's in Charge Here?" Institutional Investor 19 (February 1985): 62-66.

508. Falloon, William. "Interview: Greta Marshall." Inter-Market 4 (June 1987): 52-59.

509. Gropper, Diane H. "Pensions: Dennis Kass Has the Last Laugh." Institutional Investor 21 (January 1987): 163-165.

510. Gropper, Diane H. "The Remaking of the Pension Officer." Institutional Investor 17 (August 1983): 97-104.

511. Gropper, Diane H. "Why It Pays to Kick the Tires." Institutional Investor 18 (August 1984): 86-90.

512. Gropper, Diane H.; Rohrer, Julie; Rosenberg, Hilary; Jansson, Solveig; and Karp, Richard. "America's Best Pension Officers." Institutional Investor 21 (July 1987): 105-124.

513. Jansson, Solveig. "Are Pension Officers Becoming More Patient?" Institutional Investor 16 (November 1982): 97-103.

514. Jansson, Solveig. "Portrait of a 21st-Century Pension Officer." Institutional Investor 16 (December 1982): 249-250, 252-260.

515. Laing, Jonathan R. "Soft Dollars and Hard Cases:
      Potential Conflicts of Interest Abound for Pension Con-
      sultants." Barron's 68 (May 16, 1988): 6-7, 28-29.

516. Landau, Peter. "Paul Miller, Partner, Miller, Anderson
      & Sherrerd." Institutional Investor 21 (June 1987):
      228-230.

517. Mattlin, Everett. "Where Does the Pension Officer Go
      from Here?" Institutional Investor 20 (August 1986):
      129-131.

518. Rohrer, J. "Why Pension Officers Quit Their Jobs."
      Institutional Investor 12 (September 1978): 27-32+.

519. Sass, Martin D. "How (Not) to Manage Your Pension
      Fund Manager." FE: The Magazine for Financial Exec-
      utives 1 (August 1985): 37-40.

PENSION PLAN FUNDING

520. Alderson, Michael J. "Unfunded Pension Liabilities and Empirical Investigation." Ph.D. dissertation, University of Illinois, 1984. 239p.

521. Allan, Harry E. "Pension Funding: How Much Is Enough?" Financial Executive 52 (October 1984): 29-32.

522. Carson-Parker, John. "Why Dark Clouds Are Gathering Over Pension Funds." Chief Executive 24 (Summer 1983): 34-40.

523. Casale, Debra A. "Unfunded Pension Liabilities: Should You Be Concerned?" Journal of Commercial Bank Lending 66 (November 1983): 2-10.

524. Cooper, Robert D. Pension Fund Operations and Expenses. Brookfield, WI: International Foundation of Employee Benefit Plans, 1980. 149p.
    A broad study of collectively bargained, multiemployer, defined benefit plans. An examination of the accounting, acturial, consulting, administrative, and legal expenses associated with pension funds is presented. Numerous tables and appendices help clarify the study's results.

525. Executive Report on Large Corporate Pension Plans. New York: Johnson & Higgins, 1978-1985. (Annual).

526. "The Falloff in Contributions." Institutional Investor 19 (January 1985): 109-112.

527. Funding Pensions: Issues and Implications for Financial Markets: Proceedings of a Conference held at Melvin Village, New Hampshire, October, 1976. Boston:

66

Public Information Center, Federal Reserve Bank of
Boston, 1976. 215p.
A collection of papers which address two fundamental
issues relating to public pension plans--first, the
impact of public pension plan underfunding on savings
and capital formation; and second, the changing age
structure of the U.S. population and its effect on
pension programs. Funding government pensions
and the impact of ERISA on pension plans are among
other topics discussed. Conferees contributing to
this work include distinguished economists Martin S.
Feldstein, James Tobin, Joseph A. Pechman, and
Randall D. Weiss.

528.   Gropper, Diane H. "How Public Funds Are Waking
Up." Institutional Investor 17 (October 1983):   227-238.

529.   Issues in Unfunded Pension Liabilities. Brookfield, WI:
International Foundation of Employee Benefit Plans,
1981. 61p.
This work examines the effects of a corporation's
pension liability on its ability to borrow, and on
the stock price. The accounting treatment of unfunded pension liabilities is also explained. Includes
a short glossary of terms and a bibliography.

530.   Johnson, Allan W., and Wilson, Hamline C. "Smaller
Plans Fight the Funding Squeeze." Pension World 21
(February 1985):   40-44, 49.

531.   Kemp, Robert S. Firm Life Cycle Effects on Pension
Funding Decisions. Brookfield, WI: International
Foundation of Employee Benefit Plans, 1984.   21p.
This brief research study identifies the factors that
influence pension funding decisions in emerging,
growing, mature, and declining firms. The statistical
measures of pension funding, a list of financial
variables, and a summary of significant correlations
are presented. Includes a bibliography.

532.   Lipkin, David M. "How Does a Plan Sponsor Choose
a Funding Method?" Pension World 21 (March 1985):
46-48.

533.   McClanahan, Donald T. Pension Plans & Pension Funding

(The Actuarial Basis) Simplified for Non-Actuaries. St.
Louis, MO: Pension Service Publishing Company, 1980.
453p.
A compendium of actuarial principles, benefit formulas,
and cost methods used in pension planning. Pension
plan administration and implementation under ERISA
is also examined. Includes tables and funding calcu-
lations.

534. Modic, Stanley J. "Pensions: Who'll Pay the Price?"
Industry Week 236 (May 16, 1988): 71-76.

535. Monnett, John A. "Pension Plans Help Prepare for the
Future." Healthcare Financial Management 37 (July
1983): 50-56.

536. Munnell, Alicia H. "Pension Contributions and the
Stock Market." New England Economic Review (Novem-
ber/December 1987): 3-14.

537. "Pension Scoreboard: A Controversial Glow of Health."
Business Week Industrial/Technology Edition (September
17, 1984): 153-160.

538. Perham, John. "Pension Plans: Problems of Plenty."
Dun's Business Month 123 (January 1984): 39-43.

539. Polisner, Dennis M. "Pension Planning: And Now, a
Word From Our Sponsors." Management Focus 31
(November/December 1984): 17-21.

540. Ring, Trudy. "Profiles: The Top 200-- '84 Payouts
Top Contributions." Pensions & Investment Age 13
(January 21, 1985): 13, 32-90.

541. Rohrer, Julie. "Big Action at the Small Funds."
Institutional Investor 18 (October 1984): 251-258.

542. Shultz, Paul T., and Klein, James P. "Reexamining
Pension Plans When Financial Circumstances Change."
Employee Relations Law Journal 9 (Summer 1983): 158-
166.

543. Smith, Kenneth R., and Phillips, Robert C. "What Is
Your Pension Funding Objective?" Financial Executive
51 (September 1983): 26-31.

544.   Sze, Man-Bing. Pension Funding Policy and Corporate
       Finance. Santa Monica, CA: Rand, 1985.

545.   Trowbridge, C. L., and Farr, C. E. The Theory and
       Practice of Pension Funding. Homewood, IL: Richard
       D. Irwin, 1976.   154p.
       A textbook summary of the basic principles, methods,
       practices, and problems associated with pension plan
       funding. Actuarial assumptions, cost methods, an-
       cillary benefits, and the regulatory environment are
       among the other related topics covered.   Includes
       a selected readings list, illustrations of actuarial
       models, and an index to the book's pension funding
       terms.

546. Adcock, G. "Coca-Cola Company: Refreshing Benefits
      Package." Pension World 15 (June 1979): 8-10+.

547. Caswell, Jerry W. "Economic Efficiency in Pension Plan
      Administration; A Study of the Construction Industry."
      Ph.D. dissertation, University of Pennsylvania, 1974.
      229p.

548. Darby, Rose. "Oil Slump Hits Industry Funds Hard."
      Pensions & Investment Age 14 (August 18, 1986): 3,
      64.

549. Derven, R[onald]. "Diversity Is Key to Pension Fund
      Growth at International Paper." Pension World 15
      (August 1979): 16-18+.

550. Derven, Ronald. "General Foods' Pension Recipe."
      Pension World 19 (December 1983): 11-13.

551. Derven, R[onald]. "United Technologies: Engineering
      a $2.3 Billion Pension Fund Portfolio." Pension World
      16 (August 1980): 12-13+.

552. Donlan, Thomas G. "Gold-Plated Steel Parachutes: How
      One Pension Fund Ran Out of Money." Barron's 66
      (December 1, 1986): 11, 26-32.

553. Drescher, N. M. "Workmen's Compensation and Pension
      Proposal in the Brewing Industry, 1910-1912: A Case
      Study in Conflicting Self-Interest." Industrial and
      Labor Relations Review 24 (October 1970): 32-46.

554. Gardner, Elizabeth. "Pension Plan Executives Labor
      to Make Changes." Modern Healthcare 18 (April 15,
      1988): 30-37.

555. Gillespie, Richard, and Rudin, Brad. "Funds Shelter Surplus." Pensions & Investment Age 14 (December 22, 1986): 1, 47.

556. Givant, Marlene. "Sterling Drug Diversifies Equity Approach." Pensions & Investment Age 15 (April 20, 1987): 4.

557. Grostoff, Steven. "LTV Pension Funds Double PBGC Deficit." National Underwriter (Property/Casualty/ Employee Benefits) 91 (January 19, 1987): 3, 50.

558. Higgins, H. K. "Honeywell: Controlling the Climate of a Pension Plan." Pension World 17 (January 1981): 13-15+.

559. Hill, Susan. "Pension Profile: Letting the Numbers Speak for Themselves." Institutional Investor 17 (December 1983): 123-127.

560. Ibrahim, Ibrahim B. "An Econometric Model for Life Insurance Companies' and Pension Funds' Investment Behavior." Ph.D. dissertation, New York University, 1969. 148p.

561. Mahar, Maggie. "Campus Rebellion: Professors Are Up in Arms About Their Retirement Fund." Barron's 67 (August 17, 1987): 6-7, 29-35.

562. Michael, Nancy M. "Processing Your Pension/Retirement Plan In-House." Business Software Review 5 (September 1986): 31-32.

563. Milligan, John W. "Pensions: When the Cheering Stops." Institutional Investor 20 (February 1986): 89-92.

564. "The 1985 Pension Olympics." Institutional Investor 19 (February 1985): 69-100.

565. "Pension Funds: Keeping the Promises, Cutting the Costs." Chemical Week 134 (May 30, 1984): 32-33.

566. Roberts, Diana H. P. "Hershey's Pension Fund--Keeping It Sweet." Pension World 18 (December 1982): 13-16.

567. Robertshaw, Nicky. "Steel Benefit Liability at Nearly
     $12 Billion." Pensions & Investment Age 15 (September
     7, 1987): 3, 77.

568. Slater, Robert Bruce. "Banks That Raided Their Pension
     Plans." Bankers Monthly 104 (March 1987): 24-26, 38.

569. "TIAA-CREF Approves Major Pension Expansion." Em-
     ployee Benefit Plan Review 42 (February 1988): 33-36.

570. Tobey, John S., and Brennan, Lawrence T. "How Much
     Is My Pension Worth?" Pension World 21 (December
     1985): 36-38.

571. Andrews, Victor L., Jr. "Investment Practices of Corporate Pension Funds." Ph.D. dissertation, Massachusetts Institute of Technology, 1958.

572. Angell, R. J., and Lindbeck, R. S. "Tax-Sheltered Retirement Plans: A Sensitivity Analysis of the Rate of Return." Business Review 29 (July 1977): 18-21.

573. Beebower, G. L., and Bergstrom, G. L. "Performance Analysis of Pension and Profit-Sharing Portfolios: 1966-1975." Financial Analysts Journal 33 (May 1977): 31-32+.

574. Beier, Elliot, ed. How to Increase the Investment Return of Pension and Welfare Funds. New York: Dornost, 1965. 72p.
    An edited collection of informative essays which feature investment portfolio strategies for public and private pension fund managers and fiduciaries. Irving L. Straus, Edward F. Baumer, Robert Burr, Jean M. Lindberg, and Daniel S. Kampel are among the experts contributing to this work.

575. Ben-Artzy, Andy. "An Analysis of Institutional Investment Performance--The Case of Pension Funds." Ph.D. dissertation, New York University, 1979. 317p.

576. Bergstrom, G. L., and Frashure, R. D. "Setting Investment Policy for Pension Funds." Sloan Management Review 18 (Spring 1977): 1-16.

577. Berkowitz, Stephen A. The Investment Performance of Corporate Pension Plans. Westport, CT: Greenwood Press, 1988. 132p.
    A study which compares corporate pension plan

73

portfolio performance with mutual funds, standard
market indexes, public employee plans, and endowment
funds. Includes an examination of pension plan
rates of return, turnover and transaction costs,
risk and return measurement, and the pension plan
portfolio asset allocation process. Supporting statistical data and mathematical formulas are provided.

578. Bleiberg, Steven D. "Pension Fund Perspective: The
Nature of the Universe." Financial Analysts Journal
42 (March/April 1986): 13-14.

579. Brinson, Gary P., et al. "A Composite Portfolio Bench-
mark for Pension Plans." Financial Analysts Journal
42 (March/April 1986): 15-24.

580. Brinson, Gary P., et al. "Determinants of Portfolio
Performance." Financial Analysts Journal 42 (July/August
1986): 39-44.

581. Brooks, John N. Conflicts of Interest: Corporate
Pension Fund Asset Management: Report to the Twentieth Century Fund Steering Committee on Conflicts
of Interest in the Securities Markets. New York:
Twentieth Century Fund, 1975. 61p.
This study briefly reports on several critical aspects
of pension fund administration, including the regulatory, and conflict of interest concerns associated
with their investment.

582. Burr, Barry B., et al. "Groups Survey Performance
Data." Pensions & Investment Age 14 (February 17,
1986): 1, 74-76.

583. Burr, Barry B. "SBA Loans Draw Pension Assets."
Pensions & Investment Age 14 (August 18, 1986): 2, 65.

584. Burroughs, Eugene B. "Asset Allocation Decisions
Affect Real Rate of Return." Pension World 20 (November 1984): 48, 54-56.

585. Burroughs, Eugene B. "A Fiduciary's List of New
Year's Resolutions." Pension World 22 (January 1986):
48-50.

586. Burroughs, Eugene B. "Setting Investment Objectives
      Is a Delicate Balancing Act." Pension World 23 (March
      1987): 56-58.

587. Burroughs, Eugene B. "Who Controls the Destiny of
      the Asset Mix?" Pension World 23 (June 1987): 56-58.

588. Cahan, Vicky, and Weiss, Stuart. "Pension Fund Score-
      board: The Huge Pension Overflow Could Make Waves
      in Washington." Business Week Industrial/Technology
      Edition (August 12, 1985): 71-75.

589. Cashman, D. V., and Farrell, J. H., Jr. "Investment
      Strategy of a Pension Plan." Financial Executive 46
      (December 1978): 20-29+.

590. Christie, Claudia M. "A Consultant Helps Companies
      Manage the Forgotten Funds." New England Business
      5 (October 3, 1983): 59-64.

591. Cohn, Richard A., and Lashgari, Malek K. "Implications
      of Uncertain Inflation for Defined Benefit Pension Plans."
      Benefits Quarterly 3 (2nd Quarter 1987): 47-51.

592. Conrad, A. "Girding Up for Another Bull Market."
      Pension World 16 (April 1980): 24-26+.

593. Cottle, Sidney. "Pension Fund Management: What's
      the Best Strategy?" Financial Executive 51 (October
      1983): 52-61.

594. Crabbe, Matthew. "US Pension Funds Follow the Boat."
      Euromoney (March 1987): 91-99.

595. Cummins, J. David, and Outreville, J. Francois. "The
      Portfolio Behavior of Pension Funds in the US: An
      Econometric Analysis of Changes Since the New Regu-
      lation of 1974." Applied Economics 16 (October 1984):
      687-701.

596. Darby, Rose. "Funds Selecting for Style." Pensions
      & Investment Age 14 (August 18, 1986): 58.

597. Davey, P. J. "Appraising Pension Fund Investment
      Performance." Conference Board Record 11 (January
      1974): 41-44.

598. Debard, Roger. "Economics of Hedging Corporate Pension
      Fund Reinvestment Rate Uncertainty." Ph.D. disserta-
      tion, Claremont Graduate School, 1981. 134p.

599. Derven, Ronald. "What Plan Sponsors Say About Venture
      Capital Today." Pension World 23 (August 1987): 26-
      28.

600. Dietz, Peter O. "Evaluating the Investment Performance
      of Noninsured Pension Funds." Ph.D. dissertation,
      Columbia University, 1965. 212p.

601. Dietz, P[eter] O. "Investment Goals; A Key to Measuring
      Performance of Pension Funds." Financial Analysts
      Journal 24 (March 1968): 133-137.

602. Dietz, Peter O. Pension Funds: Measuring Investment
      Performance. New York: Free Press, 1966. 166p.
      This timely study provides a method for evaluating
      the investment performance of noninsured private
      pension funds. The performance measurement of
      strategic decisions, investment timing, the considera-
      tion of the evaluation model, and the obligations of
      fund managers are among the noteworthy areas ex-
      amined. Footnoted and explanatory references, plus
      a bibliography, are provided.

603. Dietz, P[eter] O., and Silliams, G. P., Jr. "Influence
      of Pension Fund Asset Valuations on Rate of Return."
      Financial Executive 38 (May 1970): 32-35.

604. Dunetz, Martin R. How to Finance Your Retirement.
      Reston, VA: Reston Pub. Co., 1979. 227p.
      This guide examines specific types of investments
      applicable for retirement programs. Corporate retire-
      ment plans, mutual fund investments, individual
      retirement accounts, public pension plans, and social
      security are among the types of retirement programs
      briefly investigated. A selected bibliography,
      glossary of terms, and performance data of securities
      associated with pension fund investments are provided.

605. Ellis, C. D. "Caution on Pension ROI Assumptions."
      Harvard Business Review 50 (July 1972): 6-8+.

606. Ellis, C[harles] D. "Investment Policies of Large Corporate Pension Funds." Ph.D. dissertation, New York University, 1979. 171p.

607. Estrella, Arturo. "Portfolio Effects of Asset Idiosyncrasies; The Cases of Money and Pensions." Ph.D. dissertation, Harvard University, 1983. 169p.

608. Falloon, William D. "Pension Funds: The World Is No Longer Flat." InterMarket 3 (December 1986): 46-50.

609. Falloon, William. "Public Pension Plans: The Liability 2000/Market Flexibility/Dynamic Mindsets and Dynamic Portfolios." InterMarket 3 (September 1986): 15-24.

610. Falloon, William. "U.S. Pension Funds Move Abroad." InterMarket 3 (November 1986): 22-28.

611. Ferris, Stephen P., and Rykaczewski, Karl P. "Social Investment and the Management of Pension Portfolios." Journal of the American Society of CLU 40 (November 1986): 60-64.

612. Fish, W. W. "Perceptions of Pension Liabilities." Governmental Finance 8 (March 1979): 29-32.

613. Fisher, E. E., and Messner, V. A. "Guide to Pension Fund Performance Measurement." Trusts & Estates 111 (February 1972): 102-105+.

614. Fiske, Heidi S. "Robert Kirby, Chairman, Capital Guardian Trust Co." Institutional Investor 21 (June 1987): 34-37.

615. Fletcher, William C. "Can A Portfolio Be Too Diversified?" Pension World 22 (April 1986): 30-33.

616. Forbes, Daniel. "Hidden Risks in Portfolio Insurance." Dun's Business Month 128 (September 1986): 34-36.

617. Foster, Ronald S. "Noninsured Corporate Pension Funds as a Source of Funds for Savings and Loan Associations." Ph.D. dissertation, Ohio State University, 1961. 289p.

618. Freelund, D. E. "Practical Approach to Pension Investments." Financial Executive 45 (August 1977): 20-25.

619. Gamlin, Joanne. "Los Angeles Center for Futures Use in Pension Funds?" Futures: The Magazine of Commodities & Options 15 (December 1986): 60-61.

620. Gamlin, Joanne. "Pension Funds Changing Attitudes Toward Futures." Futures: The Magazine of Commodities & Options 15 (August 1986): 42-43, 46.

621. Gillio, Matthew. "Choosing the Right Money Manager for Portfolio Investment." Healthcare Financial Management 40 (December 1986): 109-110.

622. Givant, Marlene. "Benefit Plans Add to Mutual Funds." Pensions & Investment Age 15 (February 9, 1987): 34.

623. Good, Walter R. "Accountability for Pension Fund Performance." Financial Analysts Journal 40 (January/February 1984): 39-42.

624. Gropper, Diane H. "The Boom in Asset-Liability Models." Institutional Investor 19 (August 1985): 97-101.

625. Gropper, Diane H. "Pensions: Drawing the Line on Fees." Institutional Investor 19 (December 1985): 90-101.

626. Grunthal, Peter F. "Pension Financing." FE: The Magazine for Financial Executives 2 (September 1986): 34-39.

627. Gumperz, J., and Page, E. W., Jr. "Misconceptions of Pension Fund Performance." Financial Analysts Journal 26 (May 1970): 30-32+.

628. Gurwin, L. "Do Interest-Rate Futures Have a Future in Pensionland?" Institutional Investor 14 (February 1980): 99-100+.

629. Hankin, Sam. "Robert Monks: Pension Funds Really Are the Owners of Corporations." Pension World 22 (May 1986): 20-26.

630. Hardaway, R., Jr. "Structuring a Multi-Employer Pension Investment Portfolio." Pension World 16 (June 1980): 27-30; (July 1980): 24-27.

631. Hardy, S. "Measuring Performance of Option Portfolios."
      Pension World 16 (June 1980): 50-53.

632. Hawthorne, Fran. "The Holistic Approach to Managing
      Pensions." Institutional Investor 18 (December 1984):
      129-134.

633. Hawthorne, Fran. "Measuring the Measurers." Insti-
      tutional Investor 19 (January 1985): 199-202.

634. Hawthorne, Fran. "Pension Management: The Dawning
      of Performance Fees." Institutional Investor 20 (Sep-
      tember 1986): 139-146.

635. Hemmerick, Steve. "Protecting Gain Small Plans' Aim."
      Pensions & Investment Age 14 (November 24, 1986):
      3, 47.

636. Hemmerick, Steve. "Sponsors Get Good Grade."
      Pensions & Investment Age 15 (June 1, 1987): 26.

637. Henderson, C. R. "More Effective and Safer Pension
      Investing." Financial Executive 48 (September 1980):
      20-23.

638. Hill, Joanne M. "Pension Fund Management: A Frame-
      work for Investment and Funding Decisions." Ph.D.
      dissertation, Syracuse University, 1978. 255p.

639. Hill, Susan. "Putting a Lid on Pension Costs." Insti-
      tutional Investor 18 (April 1984): 115-119.

640. Hollister, Robert L., Jr. "Public Pension Funds Venture
      Capital Investment." Governmental Finance 12 (Septem-
      ber 1983): 17-20.

641. Howard, Lisa S. "Pension Planners Picking Old Standbys
      for Funding." National Underwriter (Life/Health/Financial
      Services) 91 (May 4, 1987): 13, 17.

642. Howell, P. L. "Re-Examination of Pension Fund Invest-
      ment Policies." Journal of Finance 13 (May 1958):
      261-274.

643. Jansson, Solveig. "Pension Management: A Tale of Two

Billionaires." Institutional Investor 21 (August 1987):
119-121.

644. Jansson, Solveig. "Portfolio Strategy--Can Style Switch-
      ing Ever Become Respectable?" Institutional Investor
      19 (October 1985): 219-222.

645. Joanette, Francois P. "Managing Corporate Pension
      Funds--A Study of the Determinants of Pension Funding
      and Assets Allocation Decisions." Ph.D. dissertation,
      University of Pennsylvania, 1985. 327p.

646. Jog, Vijay M. "Essays on the Financial Management of
      Pension Funds." Ph.D. dissertation, McGill University,
      1983.

647. Kao, Duen-Li. "Managing Cash Balances for Corporate
      Pension Funds." Journal of Cash Management 6
      (November/December 1986): 68-74.

648. Kendrick, Clinton J. "Is It Time for Pension Funds to
      Invest Globally?" Pension World 23 (April 1987): 22-24,
      28.

649. Kopp, B. "Managing Pension Portfolios to Meet Increasing
      Future Costs." Commercial and Financial Chronicle 212
      (August 13, 1970): 431+.

650. Kopp, B. S. "Quick! Tell Me How to Monitor Investment
      Performance." Pension World 13 (February 1977): 37-
      40.

651. Krauss, Alan. "Funds Keeping Nest Eggs Away from
      'Vulture' Pools." Pensions & Investment Age 14 (March
      31, 1986): 13-14.

652. Kritzman, Mark. "What's Wrong with Portfolio Insurance?"
      Journal of Portfolio Management 13 (Fall 1986): 13-16.

653. Large Corporate Pensions; Report to Participants.
      Greenwich, CT: Greenwich Associates, 1973- . (An-
      nual).
           A research report which assesses the fund management
      practices, investment strategies, and policy considera-
      tions associated with private pension funds in the

United States. Report features include an interview with the study's consultants, a list of actuarial assumptions made, and the work's findings.

654. Leibowitz, Martin L. "The Dedicated Bond Portfolio in Pension Funds--Part 1: Motivation and Basics." Financial Analysts Journal 42 (January/February 1986): 68-75.

655. Leibowitz, Martin L. "Pension Asset Allocation Through Surplus Management." Financial Analysts Journal 43 (March/April 1987): 29-40.

656. Lerner, Eugene M. "What Investment Style Works Best for a Small Fund?" Pension World 23 (May 1987): 47-48.

657. Litvak, Lawrence. "Pension Funds & Economic Renewal." Mortgage Banking 43 (January 1983): 28-33.

658. Lofgren, Eric P. "Portfolio Insurance: An Actuary's Perspective." Journal of Pension Planning & Compliance 12 (Winter 1986): 349-357.

659. Malca, Edward. Bank-Administered, Commingled Pension Funds: Performance and Characteristics, 1962-1970. Lexington, MA: Lexington Books, 1973. 93p.
A work which examines the characteristics of selected non-insured private pension funds. Investment performance and portfolio evaluation theory are explicated. Includes numerous charts, statistical tables, and explanatory references.

660. Malca, Edward. Pension Funds and Other Institutional Investors: Performance and Evaluation. Lexington, MA: Lexington Books, 1975. 140p.
This statistical analysis quantifies fund performance and investment returns. Time series data, fund volatility, rates of return, and asset distribution figures are presented in numerous charts and tables.

661. Malley, Susan L., and Jayson, Susan. "Why Do Financial Executives Manage Funds the Way They Do?" Financial Analysts Journal 42 (November/December 1986): 56-62.

662. Margotta, Donald. "The Effect of Institutional Ownership of Shares on Financial Decisions of the Firm." Ph.D. dissertation, University of North Carolina at Chapel Hill, 1984. 174p.

663. Marshall, James N., II. "The Pension Fund Asset Mix Decision in a World of Economic Uncertainty: A Simulation Approach." Ph.D. dissertation, Lehigh University, 1982. 121p.

664. Marshall, Stanmore B. "Fixed-Income Securities in the Pension Fund: The Effect on Market Valuation." D.B.A. dissertation, University of Virginia, 1986. 201p.

665. Mattlin, Everett. "Portfolio Strategy: The Best of Both Worlds." Institutional Investor 20 (September 1986): 173, 176.

666. Mazzella, Donald P. "Funds Lag in Going On-Line/ Data Bases." Pensions & Investment Age 12 (October 1, 1984): 16-43.

667. McGoldrick, Beth. "Inside the Big In-House Funds." Institutional Investor 17 (November 1983): 137-155.

668. Melone, Victor J. "Pension Funds: Balance Your Bond/Stock Investments." Financial Executive 52 (March 1984): 17-24.

669. Much, Marilyn. "Pension Insurance?" Industry Week 230 (September 1, 1986): 26-27.

670. Munnell, Alicia H. "Who Should Manage the Assets of Collectively Bargained Pension Plans?" New England Economic Review (July/August 1983): 18-30.

671. Murray, R. F. "Yardstick to Measure Pension Fund Performance." Banking 61 (June 1969): 59+.

672. Murray, Thomas J. "Venturesome Pension Funds." Dun's Business Month 121 (January 1983): 64-66.

673. "The 1986 Pension Olympics." Institutional Investor 20 (February 1986): 95-135.

674. "Opportunities in Pension Investment Future." Employee
      Benefit Plan Review 42 (July 1987): 40-44.

675. Parker, Marcia. "Consultant Pools Showing Steady
      Growth in Assets." Pensions & Investment Age 15 (May
      25, 1987): 4, 138.

676. Parker, Marcia. "Strategy Integration Comes Under
      Debate." Pensions & Investment Age 15 (April 20, 1987):
      3, 54-55.

677. Pasucci, John J. "The Investment Policies of Collectively
      Bargained Pension Funds." Ph.D. dissertation, Stanford
      University, 1964. 294p.

678. Pearlman, Ellen. "The 1983 Pension Olympics." Insti-
      tutional Investor 17 (February 1983): 94-122.

679. Peers, Michael R. "Smaller Plans Can Invest Internation-
      ally with Mutual Funds." Pension World 22 (December
      1986): 30, 32.

680. "Pension Management: A Face-Lift for the Big Insurers."
      Institutional Investor 18 (June 1984): 129-135.

681. "Pension Management: The 1987 Pension Olympics."
      Institutional Investor 21 (February 1987): 89-127.

682. "Performance Statistics: Investment Counselors."
      Pension World 13 (February 1977): 28-31.

683. Polverini, Leo J., Jr. "Portfolio Insurance Controls
      Equity Risk for Plan Sponsors." Journal of Compensation
      & Benefits 3 (July/August 1987): 29-32.

684. Polverini, Leo J., Jr. "Recipe for Pension Investment:
      Mix Assets Well." Cash Flow 7 (December 1986): 32-35.

685. "Portfolio Strategy: Keeping Ahead of the Spinning
      Sectors." Institutional Investor 18 (June 1984): 137-
      144.

686. Richards, Thomas M., and McPike, Nancy E. "Bench-
      mark Portfolios: Crafting a Valid Yardstick." Cash
      Flow 8 (February 1987): 47-48.

687. Ring, Trudy. "Funds Not Rushing to Discounters:
      Pension Executives Prefer to Stick with Institutional
      Brokers." Pensions & Investment Age 15 (September
      1987): 31.

688. Ring, Trudy. "Venture Maze Has Many Paths." Pensions
      & Investment Age 15 (July 1987): 19.

689. Rohrer, Julie. "The Great Debate Over Performance
      Fees." Institutional Investor 17 (November 1983): 123-
      130.

690. Rohrer, Julie. "The 1984 Pension Olympics." Institu-
      tional Investor 18 (February 1984): 76-112.

691. Rohrer, Julie. "The Pension Management Party Is Over."
      Institutional Investor 8 (November 1984): 61-68.

692. Rohrer, Julie "Pension Management: The Pride of Bala
      Cynwyd." Institutional Investor 21 (April 1987): 124-
      131.

693. Roscow, J. P. "Are the Pension Funds Hurting Your
      Portfolio?" Financial World 142 (July 31, 1974): 11-13.

694. Rosenberg, Hilary. "Invasion of the Investment Banks."
      Institutional Investor 21 (September 1987): 117-124.

695. Rudd, Andrew. "Portfolio Management: International
      Investing." Journal of Accounting, Auditing & Finance
      9 (Fall 1985): 89-96.

696. Rybke, John S. "Pension Parachutes: More Weapons
      in Your Arsenal to Ward Off a Hostile Takeover." FE:
      The Magazine for Financial Executives 2 (November
      1986): 31-33.

697. Sass, Martin D. "Bonds in the Context of the Total
      Portfolio." Pension World 20 (May 1984): 37-39.

698. Schneid, D. L. "On Measuring Pension Fund Perform-
      ance." Burroughs Clearing House 55 (April 1971):
      22-23+.

699. Schwimmer, Martin J. Pension and Institutional Portfolio

Management. New York: Praeger, 1976. 136p.
A study designed to help pension fund managers
better administer their plans. Pension fund performance, the Pension Reform Act of 1974, portfolio
strategies, and the standardization of risk and portfolio selection are among the topics covered. A brief
bibliography is included.

700. Scott, Harold W. "The Investment of Trusteed Pension
Funds." Ph.D. dissertation, New York University, 1959.

701. Seyed-Kazemi, Mohammad H. "A Comparison of Relative
Rates of Return on Private and Public Pension Funds."
Ph.D. dissertation, Clark University, 1983. 107p.

702. Sieff, J. A. "Measuring Investment Performance; The
Unit Approach." Financial Analysts Journal 22 (July
1966): 93-99.

703. Simpson, J. C. "Private Placements and the Pension
Portfolio." Pension World 13 (August 1977): 44-48.

704. Smith, R. F., and Richards, T. M. "Asset Mix and Investment Strategy." Financial Analysts Journal 32 (March
1976): 67-71.

705. Somes, Steven P., and Zurack, Mark A. "Pension
Plans, Portfolio Insurance and FASB Statement No. 87:
An Old Risk in a New Light." Financial Analysts Journal
43 (January/February 1987): 10-13.

706. Sower, John. "Using Pension Funds for Business
Financing Programs." Economic Development Review
5 (Winter 1987): 20-22.

707. Spak, Jude J. "Overfunded Plans." FE: The Magazine
for Financial Executives 2 (November 1986): 29-30.

708, "Study Confirms Funds Lag Index." Pensions & Investment Age 14 (September 29, 1986): 63.

709. "Study Shows Pension Plans Have High Degree of
Security." Best's Review Life/Health Insurance Edition
70 (June 1969): 22+.

710. Surz, Ronald J. "A Framework for Pension Investment
      Decision-Making." Pension World 19 (January 1983):
      51-56.

711. Szala, Ginger. "How Pension Fund Managers Look at
      'Insurance' Tools." Futures: The Magazine of Com-
      modities & Options 16 (April 1987): 48-49.

712. Tavel, M. K. "Can Pension Funds Beat the Market?"
      Pension World 16 (February 1980): 37-40.

713. Tepper, Irwin. "Risk vs. Return in Pension Fund In-
      vestment." Harvard Business Review 55 (March/April
      1977): 100-107.

714. Thompson, Brian C. "A Dynamic Programming Approach
      to the Pension Fund Asset Structure Problem." Ph.D.
      dissertation, Southern Methodist University, 1974. 188p.

715. Trainer, Francis H., Jr., et al. "A Systematic Approach
      to Bond Management in Pension Funds." Journal of
      Portfolio Management 10 (Spring 1984): 30-35.

716. Treynor, J. L. "How to Rate Management of Investment
      Funds." Harvard Business Review 43 (January 1965):
      63-75.

717. Treynor, J. L. "Principles of Corporate Pension Finance."
      Journal of Finance 32 (May 1977): 627-638.

718. Tyndall, D. G. "Decision Rule for Determining Pension
      and Endowment Funds' Portfolio Mix." California Manage-
      ment Review 12 (Summer 1970): 43-52.

719. Van Etten, Richard. "Active Asset Allocation Can Add
      Value to Portfolio." Employee Benefits Journal 8 (Decem-
      ber 1983): 19-21.

720. Vitarello, James D., and Saunders, George. "Pension
      Funds Use Local Banks to Invest in Small Business."
      Employee Benefits Journal 9 (March 1984): 2-6, 9.

721. Voorheis, F. L. "How Well Do Banks Manage Pooled
      Pension Portfolios?" Financial Analysts Journal 32
      (September 1976): 35-40.

722. Ward, James. "Pension Protection: New Techniques to Help Safeguard Your Plan's Assets." FE: The Magazine for Financial Executives 3 (February 1987): 34-36.

723. Warters, D. N., and Rae, W. M. "Common Stocks Poor Bet for Pension Funds." National Underwriter Life & Health Insurance Edition 63 (November 14, 1959): 14, 21, 28.

724. White, R. "Venture Capital Investments--Do They Have a Future in Pension Portfolios?" Pension World 15 (May 1979): 14-16+.

725. Williams, Christopher C. "The Managers of Those Mega-buck Pension Funds." Black Enterprise 18 (April 1988): 50-60.

726. Williams, Fred. "Internal Assets Grow 21.4% During Period." Pensions & Investment Age 15 (January 26, 1987): 16, 76.

727. Williams, Fred. "Pension Consulting Nearing a Cross-roads." Pensions & Investment Age 14 (November 10, 1986): 39, 57-58.

728. Wilson, P. N. "Danger Ahead for CFOs--Pension Fund Assets Are Fast Catching Up to Corporate Worth." Financial Executive 47 (August 1979): 11-17.

729. Wilson, P. N. "Do Pension Fund Portfolio Managers Earn Their Keep?" Pension World 13 (February 1977): 13-16+.

730. Zorn, Werner P. "Public Pension Policy: A Survey of Current Practices (Part 1)." Governmental Finance 12 (September 1983): 3-6.

731. Aaron, Benjamin. Legal Status of Employee Benefit
     Rights under Private Pension Plans. Homewood, IL:
     Richard D. Irwin, Inc., 1961. 130p.
     This report investigates common law and statutory
     rules which protect benefit rights in the United
     States. The establishment, operation and regulation
     of private pension plans is also examined. Includes
     an index to relevant court cases.

732. Allan, Harry E. "Recent Developments in Private
     Pensions." Management Review 76 (January 1987): 54-55.

733. Bartlett, D. K., 3rd, and Schreitmueller, R. G.
     "Private Pensions: An Agenda for the 1980s." Best's
     Review Life/Health Edition 81 (May 1980): 30+.

734. Bell, Donald, and Braham, Avy. "Surviving Spouse's
     Benefits in Private Pension Plans." Monthly Labor Review
     107 (April 1984): 23-31.

735. Bodie, Zvi, ed. Issues in Pension Economics. Chicago:
     University of Chicago Press, 1987. 376p.
     A collection of papers presented at a 1984 NBER
     conference which explore corporate pension policy,
     unfunded pension liabilities, pension inequality, and
     pension plan integration. Michael J. Boskin, Alan
     J. Marcus, R. Glenn Hubbard, and Jeremy I. Bulow
     are among the professors contributing to the confer-
     ence. Includes actuarial formulas and supporting
     demographic data.

736. Boynton, E. F., and Mahoney, M. J. "Private Pension
     Plans and Social Security Integration." Pension World
     14 (October 1978): 52-56.

737. Bratter, H. "Private Pension Funds; a Growing Giant."
      Banking 52 (December 1959): 43-56.

738. Burrows, E. E. "Private Pension Plans: Why Congress
      Isn't Going Far Enough." Financial Executive 42 (April
      1974): 80-82+.

739. Bussewitz, Walter. "Private Pensions: Where Are They
      Going?" Life Association News 81 (August 1986): 25-31.

740. "Cite Private Pensions as Success Story." National
      Underwriter Property & Casualty Insurance Edition 85
      (January 23, 1981): 28-30.

741. Cochran, J. R. "Private Pension Plans: Security or
      Boon-Doggle?" Administrative Management 32 (March
      1971): 26-28.

742. Corpus, Janet M. "Private Old-Age Pensions; A Study
      of Corporate Needs and Social Welfare." Ph.D. disserta-
      tion, Massachusetts Institute of Technology, 1980.

743. Cummings, F. "Private Pensions: The Case for Reason-
      able Reform." Financial Executive 41 (May 1973): 25-31.

744. Cymrot, Donald J. "An Economic Analysis of Private
      Pensions...." Ph.D. dissertation, Brown University,
      1978. 176p.

745. [No Entry]

746. Da Motta, Luiz F. "Multiperiod Contingent Claim Models
      with Stochastic Exercise Prices: An Application to
      Pension Fund Liability Insurance and Valuation of Firms."
      Ph.D. dissertation, University of Southern California,
      1979.

747. Davis, Edward H. "Something New for Negotiated Hourly
      Pension Plans." Pension World 13 (November 1977):
      47-50.

748. Davis, H. E., and Strasser, A. "Private Pension Plans,
      1960 to 1969--An Overview." Monthly Labor Review 93
      (July 1970): 45-56.

749.   Davis, R. "Big Firms Take New Approaches to Plan
       Design." Pension World 15 (April 1979): 16-18.

750.   Delaney, Michael M. "Integration of Private Pension
       Plans with Social Security." Ph.D. dissertation, Univer-
       sity of Pennsylvania, 1976. 203p.

751.   "Effects of Private Pension Plans on Labor Mobility."
       Monthly Labor Review 86 (March 1963): 285-288.

752.   "83% in Medium, Large Firms Have Pensions/Government
       Study Notes Swing to Comprehensive Coverage, Says
       Cost Containment Is Responsible." Employee Benefit
       Plan Review 39 (November 1984): 60-64, 95-102.

753.   Elebash, Clarence C., and Christiansen, William A.
       "Why Do Private Pension Funds Avoid Mortgage-Related
       Securities?" Benefits Quarterly 2 (4th Quarter 1986):
       41-48.

754.   Erlenborn, John N. "A New Beginning on the Horizon
       for Pensions." Labor Law Review 33 (June 1982):   323-
       327.

755.   Feist, William R. "The Impact of Unvested Pension
       Fund Liabilities and Surpluses on the Market Values of
       Corporations: A Cross-Sectional Sensitivity Analysis."
       Ph.D. dissertation, Temple University, 1987. 144p.

756.   Francis, Jere R., and Reiter, Sara A. "Determinants
       of Corporate Pension Funding Strategy." Journal of
       Accounting & Economics 9 (April 1987): 33-59.

757.   "Future of Private Pension Plans." Financial Executive
       43 (July 1975): 60-64.

758.   Galper, Jeffry H. "Private Pension Plans; Determinants
       of Benefit Receipt and Amount." Ph.D. dissertation,
       Bryn Mawr College, 1972. 302p.

759.   Hanrahan, I. M. "Compulsory Private Pension Plans--
       The Wave of the Future." Pension World 14 (October
       1978): 44-46+.

760.   Hendricks, H. H. "Can Private Pension Plans Measure

Up to Expectations?" <u>Personnel Journal</u> 50 (April 1971): 293-295.

761. "Inflation Is Wrecking the Private Pension System." <u>Business Week</u> (May 12, 1980): 92-96+.

762. Jackson, Paul H. "Will Private Pensions Be Legislated to Extinction?" <u>Journal of Compensation & Benefits</u> 3 (July/August 1987): 62-65.

763. Jones, David C. "Insured Pension Funds Still Losing Ground." <u>National Underwriter (Life/Health/Financial Services)</u> 91 (March 9, 1987): 25.

764. Kolodrubetz, W. W. "Private Retirement Benefits and Relationship to Earnings; Survey of New Beneficiaries." <u>Social Security Bulletin</u> 36 (Mary 1973): 16-37.

765. Landen, R. W. "Private Pensions--Guarantee or Gamble?" <u>Financial Executive</u> 41 (September 1973): 70-72+.

766. Ledolter, Johannes, and Power, Mark L. "A Study of ERISA's Impact on Private Retirement Plan Growth." <u>Journal of Risk & Insurance</u> 51 (June 1984): 225-243.

767. Leo, Mario. <u>Financial Aspects of Private Pension Plans.</u> New York: Financial Executives Research Foundation, 1975. 283p.
     A work intended to assist company executives more effectively discharge those responsibilities relating to the financial management of pensions. Financial planning, investment objectives, disclosure require- ments, and the role of the financial executive in managing pension funds are key areas covered. The questionnaire sample used and the US pension data are included in the work.

768. Mactas, L. "How Private Pension Funds Can Help Troubled Cities and States." <u>Pension World</u> 12 (October 1976): 49-50+.

769. "Massive Study on Private Pension Soundness Gives Good Report." <u>Insurance</u> 70 (April 26, 1969): 3+.

770. McGill, Dan. Fundamentals of Private Pensions. 5th ed.

Homewood, IL: Dow Jones-Irwin, 1984. 754p.
A leading textbook compendium of U.S. pension fund
investment and planning. Pension investment, plan
coverage and participation, benefit provision, and
actuarial methods are among the areas examined.
Includes numerous statistical tables and footnoted
references.

771. Mennis, Edmund A. Understanding Corporate Pension
      Plans. Charlottesville, VA: Financial Analysts Research
      Foundation, 1983. 81p.
          A guide intended to help managers better understand
      and evaluate employee benefit plans, pension invest-
      ment policies, asset valuation methods, and primary
      actuarial functions. Administrative aspective of a
      large company's benefit structure are also examined.
      A glossary of relevant terms and a checklist to assist
      corporate plan sponsors review the books' materials
      are included.

772. Mischo, William J. Corporate Pension Plan Study. A
      Guide for the 1980s. New York: Bankers Trust Co.,
      1980. 361p.
          This extensive work surveys the pension plans of
      8.2 million workers in 55 major industries. The eli-
      gibility, vesting, early retirement, and disability
      provisions of 325 pension plans are briefly noted.
      Two hundred and forty companies are represented
      in the study.

773. Mitchell, Olivia S. "The Future of Employer-Provided
      Pensions." Compensation & Benefits Mgmt 4 (Spring
      1988): 207-210.

774. Pension and Profit Sharing Plans for Small or Medium
      Size Businesses. Greenvale, NY: Panel Publishers,
      1984-   . (Quarterly).
          A one-volume loose-leaf service which clarifies and
      explains current rulings, regulations, court decisions
      and legislation affecting plans with fewer than 250
      participants. The impact of those tax reform changes
      which have taken place during the last several years
      are also reviewed. Includes a glossary of terms, in-
      formation on Employee Stock Ownership Plans (ESOPs),
      plan termination rules, and minimum funding stand-
      ards.

775. "Pensions and Profit Sharing Plans: Essential Design
      Objectives." Small Business Report 10 (December 1985):
      52-56.

776. "Performance Is the Bottom Line: TUCS Representatives
      Speak Out." Pension World 21 (September 1985): 40-
      45, 88.

777. Pesando, James E. "Discontinuities in Pension Benefit
      Formulas and the Spot Model of the Labor Market: Im-
      plications for Financial Economists." Economic Inquiry
      25 (April 1987): 215-238.

778. Rose, P. J. "Some Aspects of Private Pension Funds
      and the Capital Market." Economic Record 43 (Septem-
      ber 1967): 354-370.

779. Schmitt, Donald G. "Postretirement Increases Under
      Private Pension Plans." Monthly Labor Review 107 (Sep-
      tember 1984): 3-8.

780. Schultz, James H. et al. "Private Pensions Fall Far
      Short of Retirement Income Levels." Monthly Labor
      Review 102 (February 1979): 28-32.

781. Slimmon, Robert F. Successful Pension Design for Small-
      to-Medium-Sized Businesses. Reston, VA: Reston
      Publishing Company, 1985.

782. Taylor, Richard L. "Importance of Private Pensions to
      Increase Sharply." Employee Benefit Plan Review 40
      (November 1985): 64-68.

783. Thomas, D. L. "Escalating Pensions; They're Mounting
      a Threat to Corporate Finances." Barrons 54 (March
      18, 1974): 3+.

784. Thompson, G. B. "Black-White Differences in Private
      Pensions: Findings Form the Retirement History
      Study." Social Security Bulletin 42 (February 1979):
      15-22.

785. Ture, Norman B. The Future of Private Pension Plans.
      Washington, DC: American Enterprise Institute for
      Public Policy Research, 1976. 128p.

This excellent overview of private pensions describes
the demographic developments and institutional changes which have affected the growth of the system
from 1940 through the mid-1970's. The impact of
social security on private savings and pension plans
is analyzed. Explanatory references and statistical
tables are included.

786. Unger, Joseph. "Simplified Employee Pensions." CPA
Journal 57 (September 1987): 82-83.

787. Wachter, Susan M., ed. Social Security and Private
Pensions. Providing for Retirement in the Twenty-First
Century. Lexington, MA: Lexington Books, 1988.
232p.
An edited collection of papers presented at the
National Press Club in 1987 by academics, government administrators, and private executives on the
current and future financial status of the elderly.
Pension policy options for the twenty-first century
and the optimal role of private and public retirement
insurance are other key topics examined. References
and explanatory notes are included for each chapter.

788. Weiss, Stuart. "Fat Pension Funds Can Make Companies
Tempting Targets." Business Week (Industrial/Tech-
nology Edition) (November 10, 1986): 106-108.

789. Wollrych, Edmund H. "Corporate Pension Funds and
Their Effects on Other Savings Institutions." Ph.D.
dissertation, Syracuse University, 1958. 234p.

790. Wrightsman, Dwayne E. "An Analysis of the Extent
of Corporate Ownership and Control by Private Pension
Funds." Ph.D. dissertation, Michigan State University,
1964. 210p.

PUBLIC (FEDERAL, STATE AND MUNICIPAL) PENSION PLANS

791. Actuarial and Economic Analysis of State and Local
      Government Pension Plans. Washington, DC: U.S.
      General Accounting Office, 1980. 45p.
      This report attempts to estimate the future outlays
      necessary for the provision of public sponsored
      pension plans. Time series data and projections of
      salary and employment levels are presented.

792. Areson, Todd W., and Kossak, Shelley E. Pension
      Issues for Local Policymakers. Washington, DC: National
      Association of Counties/National League of Cities, 1980.
      46p.
      A handbook which summarizes how pension systems
      are administered in the public sector. Topics outlined
      include benefit provision, financing arrangements,
      actuarial funding, fiduciary responsibilities, and the
      management of pension assets. A brief, annotated
      bibliography and a glossary of terms are provided
      in the work's appendices.

793. Arnold, Frank S. "State and Local Employee Pension
      Funding Theory, Evidence, and Implications." Ph.D.
      dissertation, Harvard University, 1983. 222p.

794. Cash, Doris C., and Buckner, Kathryn C. "Salary
      Reduction Plans Benefit Public Employees, Too." Pension
      World 20 (August 1984): 28-48.

795. Eagleton, T. F. "Runaway Public Pension Systems."
      Conference Board Record 13 (April 1976): 22-24.

796. Elebash, Clarence C. "Investment Qualifications of
      State Pension Fund Trustees." Employee Benefits Journal
      9 (September 1984): 2-7.

797. Elebash, Clarence C. "Mortgage-Backed Securities Win

Support from Public Pension Funds." Pension World
23 (August 1987):   22-25, 28.

798.   "Eleventh Annual Survey of State Retirement Systems."
       Pension World 20 (August 1984):   35-47.

799.   Friend, Edward H., and Rattigan, Ellen.   "The Changing
       Profile of Public Pension Plans."   Governmental Finance
       12 (September 1983):   37-41.

800.   Gasper, Juli-Ann, and Schweig, Barry B.   "An Examina-
       tion of the Wages of Public Higher Education Employees
       and the Characteristics of Their Defined Benefit Pension
       Plans: Are There Clear Winners and Losers?"   Benefits
       Quarterly 3 (2nd Quarter 1987):   37-46.

801.   Gilbert, Gerald, and Price, Dennis.   "Georgia System
       Masters a Mountain of Paperwork."   Pension World 22
       (September 1986):   60-62, 75.

802.   Greenwald, Judy.   "Federal Workers Receive New Pension
       Plan."   Business Insurance 21 (January 5, 1987):   3, 6.

803.   Gropper, Diane H., and Swain, Alan C.   "Pensions:
       How Public Funds Are Cleaning Up Their Act."   Insti-
       tutional Investor 20 (July 1986):   117-125.

804.   Grosskopf, Shawna, et al.   "Supply and Demand Effects
       of Underfunding of Pensions on Public Employee Wages."
       Southern Economic Journal 51 (January 1985):   745-753.

805.   Hawthorne, Fran.   "The Battle of Sacramento."   Insti-
       tutional Investor 19 (June 1985):   150-163.

806.   Hayne, Catherine C., ed.   Public Employee Benefit Plans.
       Brookfield, WI: International Foundation of Employee
       Benefit Plans, 1984.   132p.
          An edited text of presentations delivered at the 1984
       Public Employees Conference by retirement system
       executives, financial managers, professors and con-
       sultants.   Pension plan design, actuarial basics, real
       estate pension investment, and retirement benefit
       adjustments are among the topics explored.   Support-
       ing expenditure, investment, and contribution data
       are provided.

807. Hemmerick, Steve. "Funds to Insure Each Other."
      Pensions & Investment Age 14 (June 23, 1986): 1, 60.

808. Hemmerick, Steve. "L.A. County Recoups $1.5 Million
      from Bank." Pensions & Investment Age 14 (September
      29, 1986): 4, 80.

809. Ippolito, Richard A. "Why Federal Workers Don't Quit."
      Journal of Human Resources 22 (Spring 1987): 281-299.

810. Jansson, Solveig. "The Private Life of Public Funds /
      The Leading Managers of Public Pension Funds." Insti-
      tutional Investor 18 (July 1984): 89-105.

811. Jump, B., Jr. "Compensating City Government Em-
      ployees: Pension Benefit Objectives, Cost Measurement,
      and Financing." National Tax Journal 29 (September
      1976): 240-256.

812. Kittrell, Alison. "Public Entity Pension Plan Assets
      Grow." Business Insurance 21 (April 13, 1987): 86.

813. Kogovsek, Raymond P. "The Public Employee Pension
      Plan Reporting and Accountability Act." Labor Law
      Journal 33 (July 1982): 387-389.

814. Krueger, James M. "Information Needed for the
      Management of Locally Administered Municipal Pension
      Funds with Indiana Municipal Pension Funds as a Specific
      Case." D.B.A. dissertation, Indiana University, 1976.
      219p.

815. Lechner, Melvin N. "The Dual Roles of the Comptroller
      of the City of New York as Chief Financial Officer of
      the City and as Manager of the City Pension Funds."
      Ph.D. dissertation, New York University, 1973. 340p.

816. Lehman, June M., ed. Public Employee Benefit Plans,
      1985. Brookfield, WI: International Foundation of Em-
      ployee Benefit Plans, 1986. 96p.
          Social investing, labor and management relations,
          corporate takeovers of pension funds, and fiduciary
          responsibilities are among the pension-related issues
          and topics explored in this edited collection of essays.
          T. Boone Pickens, Robert D. Klausner, Alicia H.
          Munnell, and Gerald W. McEntee are several of the
          work's contributors.

817.   Lehrer, Brian. "Public Funds: Plans Find Ways to
       Bolster Funding." Pensions & Investment Age 14 (Octo-
       ber 13, 1986): 15-16.

818.   Leibig, M. T., and Kalman, R. W. "How Much Federal
       Regulation Do Public Funds Need?" Pension World 14
       (August 1978): 22-26.

819.   Mackin, John P. "Public Pensions in the Year 2000."
       Employee Benefits Journal 12 (March 1987): 19-23.

820.   Marks, Barry R., and Raman, Krishnamurthy K. "The
       Importance of Pension Data for Municipal and State
       Creditor Decisions: Replication and Extensions." Journal
       of Accounting Research 23 (Autumn 1985): 878-886.

821.   Murrmann, Kent F. et al. "Social Investing by State
       Public Employee Pension Funds." Labor Law Journal
       35 (June 1984): 360-367.

822.   O'Leary, Harold E. "An Analysis of the Composition,
       Operating Characteristics, and Performance of Trustee
       Managed Municipal Pension Funds in Florida." D.B.A.
       dissertation, Florida State University, 1980. 214p.

823.   Parker, Richard. Strategic Investment: Alternative
       for Public Funds. Berkeley, CA: Strategic Investment
       Advisors, 1979. 32p.
          This brief work, intended for pension managers,
       develops a portfolio approach which combines social
       responsibility and profitability as compatible invest-
       ment criteria.

824.   Pension Commission Clearinghouse. Report on State
       Pension Commissions. 9th ed. New York: Foster
       Higgins, 1988. 54p.
          A state by state summary of public employee pension
       plan coverage. The impact of federal legislation on
       state sponsored pensions is noted. Includes a
       directory list of state pension commissions.

825.   Petersen, John E. Alternative Investing by State and
       Local Pension Funds: Case Studies. Washington, DC:
       Government Finance Research Center; Municipal Finance
       Officers Association, 1980. 126p.

Massachusetts. Florida, Hawaii, Minnesota, New Hampshire, and Alabama are among the geographic sites
used for these case studies. Background information
on each public pension fund studied is provided.
Includes footnoted references and "source lists" for
each chapter.

826. Petersen, John E. Alternative Investing by State and
Local Pension Funds: Concepts, Issues and Policies.
Washington, DC: Government Finance Officers Association, 1980. 82p.
This paper explores the policy options available for
nontraditional pension fund investment. The major
concepts and issues associated with nonfinancial investment are explored.

827. Petersen, John E. Alternative Investing by State and
Local Pension Funds: Surveys of Current Practices.
Washington, DC: Government Finance Research Center;
Municipal Finance Officers Association, 1980. 55p.
A brief study which examines the major concepts
and issues pertaining to socially useful pension fund
investment. A policy option review of nontraditional
fund investment is presented. Case study surveys
of state sponsored pension fund investment practices
are also included.

828. Petersen, John E. Public Pension System Financial
Disclosure. Washington, DC: Government Finance
Research Center, 1980. 56p.
The principal users of pension disclosure information,
the kinds of financial information required, the instru-
ments of disclosure, and generally accepted accounting
procedures in effect are identified in this working
paper. Includes tables, exhibits, and explanatory
references.

829. Petersen, John E. State and Local Pension Fund Investment Performance. Washington, DC: Government
Finance Research Center, Municipal Finance Officers
Association, 1980. 100p.
A report which investigates the relationship between
the structural and procedural characteristics of
state and local pension systems. Trends in investment and rates of return are examined. Explanatory

references, tables, and mathematical formulas are
provided.

830. Petersen, John E. A Summary of State and Local
Government Public Employee Retirement System Investment
Practices and Policies. Washington, DC: Government
Finance Research Center; Municipal Finance Officers
Association, 1980. 163p.
This working paper summarizes the findings of a
two-year study of employee retirement system investments and financial disclosure practices. The results
of a 98 system survey of public employee pensions
are presented. Appendices include average composition pension portfolio information, a list of the
systems surveyed, and a copy of the questionnaire
used to gather data.

831. Polakoff, M. E. "Public Pension Funds; Past Performance and Future Opportunities." Financial Analysts
Journal 22 (May 1966): 75-81.

832. "Police and Fire Pension Systems--Colorado's Experience."
Pension World 15 (June 1979): 28-30.

833. Ruhe, Linda S. "Public Pension Funds Fuel $73 Billion
Growth/US and Canadian Master Trust Banks: Profiles."
Pensions & Investment Age 11 (June 27, 1983): 15-28.

834. "6th Annual Survey of Municipal Employee Retirement
Systems." Pension World 15 (April 1979): 52-67.

835. Thomas, W. S. "Analysis of Pension Cost for Municipalities." National Tax Journal 29 (September 1976):
234-239.

836. Thompson, William N. "Public Pension Plans: The Need
for Scrutiny and Control." Public Personnel Management
6 (July/August 1977): 203-224.

837. Tilove, Robert. Public Employee Pension Funds. New
York: Columbia University Press, 1976. 370p.

838. Blakely, Edward J., et al. "Creating Jobs Through Pension Fund Investments in Real Estate: Innovations from California." California Management Review 27 (Summer 1985): 184-197.

839. Chandor, Jeffrey F. "Pension Funds: What Are They Looking for?" Mortgage Banking 43 (November 1982): 25-30.

840. Cole, Rebel; Guilkey, David; and Miles, Mike. "Pension Fund Investment Managers' Unit Values Deserve Confidence." Real Estate Review 17 (Spring 1987): 84-89.

841. Davis, G. Abbott. "Pension Plans Should Not Form Their Own Real Estate Organizations." Real Estate Review 13 (Spring 1983): 101-106.

842. DellaGrotta, S. Q. "Investment Advice: Orchestrating the Elements." Mortgage Banking 43 (April 1983): 64-74.

843. DellaGrotta, S. Q. "Pension Funds Unlimited: Who Calls on Whom?" Mortgage Banking 45 (February 1985): 71-76.

844. Dungey, Denise M. "Pension Fund Investment in the '80s: Unprecendented [sic] Potential for Property Managers." Journal of Property Management 47 (March/April 1982): 20-21.

845. Eagle, B. "Real Estate's Overture to Pension Funds: Delayed But Moving Right Along." Pension World 16 (July 1980): 45-48.

846. Floyd, Charles F., and Wakeley, Nicholas. "Pension

Funds and the Future of the Independent Developer:
Will America Follow the British Experience?" Real Estate
Issues 8 (Spring/Summer 1983): 8-11.

847. Freeman, Louis S., and Baker, Pamela. "Pension Investments in Real Estate." Journal of Taxation of Investments 1 (Winter 1984): 155-169.

848. Garrigan, Richard T., and Young, Michael S. "The
Role of Real Estate in a Pension Fund's Mixed-Asset
Portfolio." Journal of Pension Planning & Compliance
9 (August 1983): 291-302.

849. Harmon, Christine. "Pension Fund Investment: An
Interview with Jerry Reinsdorf." Journal of Property
Management 47 (November 1982): 6-7.

850. Harmon, Christine. "Working with Pension Fund In-
vestment: An Interview with Patrick Martin and Thomas
Steel." Journal of Property Management 47 (July/
August 1982): 8-9.

851. Hemmerick, Steve. "More Funds Moving into Apartment
Market." Pensions & Investment Age 14 (October 27,
1986): 27-30.

852. Hemmerick, Steve. "Theories on How a Tight Market
Gets Tighter: Good Property Is Hard to Find/Foreign
Players Drive Up Prices." Pensions & Investment Age
15 (July 1987): 25-27.

853. Huberty, Bill. "Pension Funds and Housing Investments."
Real Estate Review 15 (Winter 1986): 103-107.

854. "Is the Syndications Boom a Blessing in Disguise for
Pension Funds?" Institutional Investor 17 (November
1983): 237-243.

855. Krauss, Alan. "Wisconsin Boosting Portfolio." Pensions
& Investment Age 13 (October 28, 1985): 49, 52.

856. McKelvy, Natalie A. Pension Fund Investments in Real
Estate: A Guide for Plan Sponsors and Real Estate
Professionals. Westport, CT: Quorum Books, 1983.
299p.

An excellent account which explains why pension fund investment is becoming an increasingly larger source of capital for the real estate market. The potential pitfalls of real estate investment/management are discussed from the perspective of a pension fund trustee. A list of the 20 largest managers of real estate equities for pension funds is provided.

857. McKelvy, Natalie. "Pension Funds: A New Source of Money for Economic Developers?" Economic Development Review 3 (Winter 1985): 48-50.

858. McMahan, John. "Measuring Real Estate Returns." Real Estate Issues 9 (Fall/Winter 1984): 33-44.

859. Miles, Mike, and Graaskamp, Jim. "Pension Fund Management: Is Small Beautiful?" Real Estate Review 14 (Spring 1984): 92-95.

860. Monks, Robert A. G. "Facilitating Pension Fund Investments in Residential Mortgages." Labor Law Journal 35 (July 1984): 387-392.

861. Munnell, Alicia H.; Blais, Lynn E.; and Keefe, Kristine M. "The Pitfalls of Social Investing: The Case of Public Pensions and Housing." New England Economic Review (September/October 1983): 20-41.

862. Napier, Thomas P., Jr. "Pension Funds: Targeting the Market." Mortgage Banking 44 (November 1983): 55-58.

863. Nelson, Jane Fant. "Pension Fund Investment in Real Estate." United States Banker 84 (May 1983): 58-60.

864. Parker, Marcia. "'Jumbos' a Big Deal for Issuers." Pensions & Investment Age 15 (August 24, 1987): 15-16.

865. "Private Pension Funds: New Source of Housing Finance?" Federal Home Loan Bank Board Journal 15 (November 1982): 9-12.

866. "Real Estate Investing by Pension Funds." Pension World 19 (September 1983): 19-31.

867. Ring, Trudy. "Investments: Adding Alternatives."
      Pensions & Investment Age. Pensions Management Mid-
      America Supplement (Spring 1987): 22-25.

868. Rosen, Kenneth T. "The Mortgage Market: High Time
      America's Pension Funds Moved In." Pension World
      11 (September 1975): 19-68.

869. Sandler, Linda. "Wall Street Enters the Pension Fray."
      Institutional Investor 16 (November 1982): 267-282.

870. Silverman, Ronald I. "Pension Funds: The 'Awakening
      Giants'." Mortgage Banking 46 (May 1986): 38-46.

871. Smedley, R. R. "Opportunity for Pension Funds: Real
      Estate Equity Development." Pension World 17 (January
      1981): 17-19.

872. Stephens, Paula S. "Pension Funds Coming Back into
      Realty Market, Following Quiet Year for Comestic, Foreign
      Investors." National Real Estate Investor 25 (September
      1983): 38-54.

873. Wellman, Leslie L., and Howe, Rex C. "Investing Pen-
      sion Assets in Real Estate." Real Estate Appraiser &
      Analyst 49 (Summer 1982): 12-17.

874. Wolf, Timothy S. "All About Pension Funds. Pension
      Fund Bibliography." Mortgage Banking 43 (November
      1982): 45-50.

875. <u>BNA Pension Reporter</u>. Washington, DC: Bureau of
National Affairs, 1975- . (Weekly).
This loose-leaf service covers current state and
national pension developments. Relevant IRS Letter
Rulings, regulatory information, court activity, and
agency opinions are summarized. Includes analysis
of important federal legislative provisions and explanations of compliance documents.

876. Boyers, Judith T. <u>Pensions in Perspective: A Guide
to Qualified Retirement Plans</u>. Cincinnati, OH: National
Underwriter Co., 1986. 227p.
This book explains government rules and regulations
that apply to pension plans. An examination of how
rules and regulations apply to the design, choice,
and implementation of qualified plans is presented.
Includes appendices of pension plan application and
registration forms.

877. <u>Compliance Guide for Plan Administrators</u>. Chicago:
Commerce Clearing House, Inc. (Biweekly).
A three-volume loose-leaf service which provides
detailed instructions for those who prepare required
ERISA disclosure reports to plan participants and
beneficiaries. Includes in-depth explanations for
all types of pension and benefit plans. Sample
ERISA forms accompanied with completed examples
are also provided.

878. <u>Guidebook to Pension Planning</u>. Chicago: Commerce
Clearing House, Inc. (Annual).
An excellent compendium of regulations and requirements that pertain to the establishment of retirement
plans. Plan approval, funding, contributions,

benefits, plan investment, administration, and profit-
sharing problems are among the many topics covered.
Includes chapters on estate planning and future
legislation.

879. Krass, Stephen J., and Keschner, Richard L. The
      Pension Answer Book. 4th ed. Greenvale, NY: Panel
      Publishers, 1988. 500p.
      An excellent guide which provides nontechnical
      information and explanations about qualified pension
      plans, relevant legal terminology, and pension funding
      requirements. Includes extensive coverage of the
      effects of the 1986 Tax Reform Act on pension
      planning and benefits. A glossary of terms and a
      separate listing of frequently asked questions are
      provided.

880. Pension Facts. Washington, DC: American Council
      of Life Insurance. (Annual).
      A leading source of statistical information on the
      distribution of pension assets, federal and private
      retirement systems, and retirement income. Time
      series pension data and a chronology of pension-
      related events from 1857 to the present are provided.
      Includes a glossary of terms and a bibliography.

881. Pension Plan Guide. Chicago: Commerce Clearing
      House, Inc. (Weekly).
      A seven-volume loose-leaf compendium of pertinent
      Internal Revenue Code provisions and regulations.
      Explanations and illustrations of how ERISA rules
      and regulations currently apply are presented. In-
      cludes information on the activities of Pension Benefit
      Guaranty Corporation (PBGC).

882. Pension and Profit Sharing. Englewood Cliffs, NJ:
      Prentice-Hall, Inc. (Weekly).
      This five-volume loose-leaf service examines the
      practical options available to plan managers and ad-
      ministrators in the establishment and development of
      pension plans. Tax Reform Act and Employee Retire-
      ment Income Security Act (ERISA) compliance re-
      quirements are explained and updated. Pre and post
      ERISA source material is provided.

883. Block, Robin S., and Cogan, Bruce A. "Pension Strategies After Norris." Journal of Pension Planning & Compliance 10 (April 1984): 131-148.

884. Buckner, Kathryn C., and Cash, Doris C. "Gender-Based Factors in Section 403(b) Plan Regulations Impose Pension and Tax Penalties on Women." Journal of Pension Planning & Compliance 10 (December 1984): 455-478.

885. Christiansen, Hanne D. "Equality and Equilibrium: Weaknesses of the Overlap Argument for Unisex Pension Plans." Journal of Risk & Insurance 50 (December 1983): 670-680.

886. "EBRI Report Finds Gender Gap in Pension Protection." National Underwriter Life and Health Insurance Edition 90 (January 4, 1986): 2.

887. Fisher, M. J. "Outlaw Pension Bias Against Women." National Underwriter Life and Health Insurance Edition 82 (April 29, 1978): 1+.

888. Franke, Ann H., and White, Lawrence. "Update on Supreme Court Litigation Over Sex-Based Actuarial Tables." Journal of Pension Planning & Compliance 8 (November 1982): 411-422.

889. "Gender Discrimination in Pension Plans." Journal of Risk and Insurance 44 (March 1977): 141-149.

890. Hickey, M. Christine. "Women and Private Pensions: Does the Proposed Legislation Eradicate Bias and Provide a Viable Source of Income?" Insurance Counsel Journal 52 (April 1985): 330-335.

891. Hickman, James C. "Pensions and Sex." Journal
      Risk & Insurance 50 (December 1983):   681-687.

892. Nagle, Robert E. "Eliminating Sex-Bias Pension
      Features After Norris: The Alternatives Available to
      Plan Sponsors." Journal of Pension Planning & Com-
      pliance 9 (October 1983):   341-356.

893. "The Unisex Dilemma." Journal of American Insurance
      60 (1984):   1-5.

894. Winston, David A. "Supreme Court Strikes Down
      Gender-Based Pensions." Life Association News 78 (Sep-
      tember 1983):   195-198.

895. Askin, Steve. "The Hidden Power of Pension Funds."
Black Enterprise 13 (January 1983): 35-37.

896. Baldwin, Stuart A., et al. Pension Funds & Ethical
Investment; A Study of Investment Practices & Oppor-
tunities, State of California Retirement Systems. New
York: Council of Economic Priorities, 1985. 191p.
This study reviews the financial, legal, and practical
considerations and consequences associated with
pension fund divestment in South Africa. The Public
Employee Retirement System, and the State Teacher
Retirement System of California are the focus of the
Council on Economic Priorities report.

897. Brauer, Mary A. "Issues to Consider in Social Investing." Pension World 19 (June 1983): 29-34.

898. Gasper, Juli-Ann, and Schweig, Barry B. "Characteristics of State Public Pension Plans That Engage in
Social Investing." Benefits Quarterly 1 (Fourth Quarter
1985): 41-50.

899. Gray, Hillel. "A New Look at Responsible Use of Pension Funds." Pension World 20 (March 1984): 25-28,
47.

900. Lanoff, I. D. "Is Social Investment of Private Pension
Plan Assets Lawful Under ERISA?" Risk Management 27
(November 1980): 26-28+.

901. Levin, Noel A., and Brossman, Mark E. "Pension Fund
Divestiture in South Africa." Employee Benefits Journal
10 (December 1985): 2-4.

902.   Levin, Noel A., and Brossman, Mark E. Social Investing
        for Pension Funds: For Love or Money. Brookfield, WI:
        International Foundation of Employee Benefit Plans, 1982.
        113p.
            This work offers practical recommendations to pension
            fund managers and fiduciaries on how to invest in
            socially useful ventures. The legal and financial
            considerations and constraints affecting social invest-
            ment practices are ascertained. Includes footnoted
            references, appendices, a subject index, and a bib-
            liography.

903.   Mares, Judith W. "Social Activism: Should It Play a
        Part in the Pension Fund Decision?" FE: The Magazine
        for Financial Executives 1 (September 1985): 43-48.

904.   McGill, Dan, ed. Social Investing. Homewood, IL:
        Richard D. Irwin, 1984. 162p.
            An edited collection of essays which address the
            issues associated with the implementation of social
            investment policy. Includes a concise examination
            of the proper allocation of decision investment power
            and the role of labor in the determination of invest-
            ment goals. Noted experts Howard Young, John H.
            Lyons, Jack Sheinkman, and Clarence C. Walton are
            among the work's contributors.

905.   Salisbury, Dallas L., ed. Should Pension Assets Be
        Managed for Social/Political Purposes?: An EBRI Policy
        Forum, December 6, 1979. Washington, DC: Employee
        Benefit Research Institute, 1980. 381p.
            A forum sponsored by the Employee Benefit Research
            Institute, which explores the social, legal, and fi-
            nancial issues associated with pension fund invest-
            ment. Lisle C. Carter, Karen Ferguson, James D.
            Hutchinson, Dallas Salisbury, and Roy A. Schotland
            are among the experts participating in the group's
            discussions. A bibliography and a short list of
            research centers which provide information on pension
            fund investment are included.

906.   Sandler, Robert N. "Social Investing--A DOL Roadmap
        for Multiemployer Plans?" Employee Benefits Journal
        9 (September 1984): 20-21, 31.

907. Zorn, Werner P. "Public Pension Policy: A Survey of
      Targeting Practices--Part 2." Governmental Finance
      12 (December 1983):   47-53.

908.   Allen, Steven G., et al. "A Comparison of Pension
       Benefit Increases and Inflation, 1973-79." Monthly Labor
       Review 107 (May 1984): 24-26.

909.   Brooks, William A. "Accounting for the Enterprise
       Pension Benefit; An Examination Based upon a Statistical
       Study of Quit Rates for 207 Pension and Nonpension
       Metropolitan Kansas City Manufacturing Firms for the
       Period, 1965-1968." Ph.D. dissertation, University of
       Kansas, 1970.   331p.

910.   Darby, Rose. "'85 Pension Assets Outpaced Liabilities."
       Pensions & Investment Age 14 (July 21, 1986):   3, 16-17,
       32.

911.   Dhaliwal, Dan S. "Measurement of Financial Leverage
       in the Presence of Unfunded Pension Obligations."
       Accounting Review 61 (October 1986):   651-661.

912.   Friedrick, Joanne. "The Mid-American Way: 'Home-
       Grown' Assets." Pensions & Investment Age. Pensions
       Management Mid-America Supplement. (Spring 1987):
       27-29.

913.   Gillespie, Richard. "Pension Assets Nearing $2 Trillion."
       Pensions & Investment Age 14 (November 24, 1986):   8.

914.   Inman, Robert P. "Public Employee Pensions and the
       Local Labor Budget." Journal of Public Economics
       19 (October 1982):   49-71.

915.   Lehrer, Brian. "Few Funds Top S&P 500 Return."
       Pensions & Investment Age 14 (November 10, 1986):
       65, 72.

916. "New Rules Would Jeopardize the Healthier Look of Pension Funds." Business Week (September 12, 1983): 126-132.

917. "91% of Workers Covered--Defined Benefit Fund Still Most Common Pension Plan." Pensions & Investment Age 14 (October 13, 1986): 60-61.

918. "Pension Fund Scoreboard--How Pension Fund Assets Grew So Quickly." Business Week (March 21, 1984): 226-228.

919. "Pension Plan Coverage Increases in Post-ERISA Era." Employee Benefit Plan Review 41 (January 1987): 61-64.

920. Phillips, S. M., and Fletcher, L. P. "Cost of Funding Benefits Under the ERISA: A Statistical Survey." Journal of Risk & Insurance 43 (December 1976): 569-585.

921. "Private Pension Plans Seen Consistently Sound." Office 101 (February 1985): 56.

922. Regan, Patrick J. "Best Pension Figures Yet." Financial Analysts Journal 39 (September/October 1983): 19-23.

923. Regan, Patrick J., and Bleiberg, Steven D. "Overfunded Pension Plans." Financial Analysts Journal 41 (November/December 1985): 10-12.

924. Survey of Actuarial Assumptions and Funding; Pension Plans with 1,000 or More Active Participants. Washington, DC: The Wyatt Co., 1969?- . (Annual).

925. "Surveys of Pooled Pension Fund Holdings." Trusts & Estates 108 (January 1969): 92-96.

926. "Top 1,000 Fund Assets Surge to $662 Billion Profiles: The Top 200." Pensions & Investment Age 11 (January 24, 1983): 1, 25-71.

927. "12th Annual Survey of Bank Pooled Pension Fund Accounts." Pension World 19 (May 1983): 43-50.

928.   Van Daniker, Relmond P., and Aldridge, C. Richard.
       "Financial Reporting for Pension Plans of Governmental
       Entities." Government Accountants Journal 33 (Winter
       1984-1985): 13-22.

929.   Webman, Nancy K. "Pension Assets Top $1 Trillion,
       Grow 24.5%." Pensions & Investment Age 14 (January
       20, 1986): 3, 97.

930.   Wiley, Carol. "Top 1,000 Funds Hit $1.3 Trillion."
       Pensions & Investment Age 15 (January 26, 1987):
       1, 20-74, 93.

931. Andrews, Emily S. "Changing Pension Policy and the Aging of America." Contemporary Policy Issues 5 (April 1987): 84-97.

932. Barrow, Tom. "Qualified Pension and Profit Sharing Plans." Insurance Sales 130 (March 1987): 37-39.

933. Bennett, Dianne. "Tax Treatment of Plan Distributions After TRA 1986." Journal of Taxation 66 (June 1987): 336-343.

934. Bertoldo, Roy. "Financing Pension Costs--Time to Reassess the Strategy." Financial Executive 51 (September 1983): 32-36.

935. Black, F. "Tax Consequences of Long-Run Pension Policy." Financial Analysts Journal 36 (July/August 1980): 21-28.

936. Burke, Francis D., Jr. "Estate Tax on Pension Death Benefits." Journal of the American Society of CLU & ChFC 41 (July 1987): 31-32.

937. Canada, Mark P. "Employees Now Face Tax When Withdrawing Their Own Contributions from a Plan." Journal of Compensation & Benefits 3 (September/October 1987): 74-79.

938. Carberry, Pauline R. "Taxation of Pension Plans for Self-Employed Individuals with Recommended Reforms." Ph.D. dissertation, Ohio State University, 1970. 175p.

939. Curtin, James B. "Disqualification of a Pension Plan: The End of the Rainbow." Journal of Pension Planning & Compliance 10 (December 1984): 429-437.

940. "Employers Change 401(k) Plans in Response to 1986
      Tax Reform Benefit Pensions." Employee Benefit Plan
      Review 42 (September 1987):   39-44.

941. Feinschreiber, Robert. "New Limits on Pension Benefits
      for Product Manufacturers." Journal of Information &
      Image Management 17 (February 1984):   36-37.

942. Fitzpatrick, Jon. "Determining If a Small Company
      Needs a Retirement Plan, and Choosing the Best Plan."
      Taxation for Accountants 35 (December 1985):   370-376.

943. Gallagher, Charles B., Jr. "New Law Imposes Strict
      Withholding Burden on Distributions from Qualified Plans."
      Taxation for Accountants 29 (November 1982):   282-285.

944. Goodman, I. "Legislative Development of the Federal
      Tax Treatment of Pension and Profit-Sharing Plans."
      Taxes 49 (April 1971):   226-249.

945. Gropper, Diane H. "Pensions: Is There Life After
      Tax Reform?" Institutional Investor 20 (December 1986):
      142-155.

946. Gropper, Diane H. "Washington's Attack on Pensions."
      Institutional Investor 19 (January 1985):   53-62.

947. Jones, David C. "Pension Review Can Lead to Profits."
      National Underwriter 91 (April 27, 1987):   14-15.

948. Lampf, S. E., and Witman, L. J. "How to Avoid the
      IRS' Strict 4-40 Vesting Requirements." Practical
      Accountant 12 (July 1979):   75-78.

949. Lowa, R. J. "Analysis of New Opportunities for Roll-
      overs of Distributions from Qualified Plans." Journal
      of Taxation 52 (February 1980):   82-85.

950. Maldonado, Kirk F. "Recent Developments Increase
      Funding Flexibility for Nonqualified Plans." Journal
      of Taxation 64 (April 1986):   216-219.

951. Margolin, Stephen M. "Pension Plans: Still the Ultimate
      Tax Shelter (Part I)." Life Association News 77
      (December 1982):   87-89.

952.   Metz, Joseph G. "Public Employee Plans and the In-
        ternal Revenue Code of 1986." Pension World 23 (August
        1987):   14-21.

953.   Metz, Joseph G. "Tax Reform '86: What Happens to
        Public Employee Plans?" Pension World 23 (January
        1987):   34-39.

954.   Mumy, Gene E., and Manson, William D. "The Relative
        Importance of Tax and Agency Incentives to Offer
        Pensions: A Test Using the Impact of ERISA." Public
        Finance Quarterly 13 (October 1985):   464-485.

955.   "Pensions! Bypassing the Street/How the New Tax Law
        Is Affecting Pension Plans." Institutional Investor
        21 (April 1987):   133-134, 139-140.

956.   Reish, C. F. "Avoid Taxation of Pension Death Bene-
        fits." Trusts & Estates 119 (February 1980):   53-58.

957.   "Responding to Pension Changes in 1986 Tax Law."
        Employee Benefit Plan Review 41 (January 1987):   15-17.

958.   Robbins, Rainard B. Impact of Taxes on Industrial
        Pension Plans. New York: Industrial Relations Coun-
        selors, 1949. 82p.
            This work briefly summarizes the historical develop-
        ment of pension plans in the United States. An
        overview of pension plan taxation from the late
        nineteenth century to the 1940s is provided. Rele-
        vant tax statutes prior to 1942 are also presented.

959.   Shawkey, Bruce. "New Tax Law Alters Retirement
        Programs." Credit Union Management 9 (November
        1986):   20, 34.

960.   Soukup, Gregory J. "Tax Planning Opportunities for
        Contributions to Pension Plans of Acquired Corporations."
        Journal of Pension Planning & Compliance 9 (February
        1983):   59-77.

961.   Stolberg, G. "Banker's Guide to Taxes on Pension Plan
        Payouts." The Bankers Magazine 162 (January 1979):
        61-64+.

962. Sugar, R. A. "Employee Contributions to Qualified
      Plans--A Frontier for Tax Planning." Taxes 57 (August
      1979): 547-552.

963. Taplin, Polly T. "Why Employee Benefits Are Target
      of Tax Increases." Employee Benefit Plan Review 42
      (July 1987): 14-16.

964. Tepper, I. "Taxation and Corporate Pension Policy."
      Journal of Finance 36 (March 1981): 1-13.

965. Tilton, J. T., and McNabb, J. A., Jr. "Complying
      with the IRS's New Guidelines for Determinations of
      Qualified Plans." Journal of Taxation 44 (January 1976):
      24-27.

966. Tracy, Thomas G., and Moore, Kim. "New Pension
      Provisions Under TEFRA." Tax Adviser 13 (December
      1982): 741-746.

967. Wiant, Elaine M., and Zwiener, Michael J. "Tax Reform
      and the Small Qualified Plan." Broker World 8 (March
      1988): 50-58.

968. Wilson, Bill C. "The 1986 Tax Reform Act: The New
      Rules for Retirement Plans." Practical Accountant 19
      (November 1986): 72-86.

969. Wisong, Wayne W. "The Plan and Uncle Sam." Associa-
      tion Management 39 (March 1987): 97-100.

970. Woyke, John F. "Current Issues in Plan Design:
      Technical Corrections Act of 1987 Answers Some Questions,
      Raises Others." Pension World 23 (September 1987):
      61-63.

971. Alderson, Michael J., and Chen, K. C. "A Survey on Current Practice in Defined Benefit Plan Terminations." Financial Analysts Journal 42 (November/December 1986): 14-18.

972. "Allocation of Assets on Termination." The CPA Journal 51 (February 1981): 86-87.

973. Beier, E. H. "Profit-Sharing and Pension Plan Termination." Monthly Labor Review 91 (July 1968): 37-40.

974. Bruinsma, James C. "When a Pension Plan Can Be Terminated Without Subjecting the Employer to Additional Liability." Taxation for Accountants 30 (January 1983): 36-43.

975. Bush, Edwin M., Jr. "Recapturing Pension Surplus: A Good Investment?" Pension World 22 (March 1986): 53-55.

976. Chadwick, G. R., Jr. "How to Terminate a Plan." Pension World 15 (June 1979): 41-42+.

977. Dankner, Harold. "Asset Reversions and Pension Plan Terminations." Corporate Accounting 3 (Winter 1985): 78-82.

978. Darby, Rose. "Academics Frown on Terminations." Pensions & Investment Age 14 (January 6, 1986): 32.

979. Estrella, Arturo. "Corporate Use of Pension Overfunding." Federal Reserve Bank of New York Quarterly Review 9 (Spring 1984): 17-25.

980. Gaver, Dean A., and Freilich, Irvin M. "Pension Plan
     Terminations: Background Implications." Pension
     World 20 (April 1984): 53-55.

981. Grubbs, Donald S., Jr. "Termination of Pension Plans
     with Asset Reversion." Journal of Pension Planning
     & Compliance 11 (Winter 1985): 229-308.

982. Hamdallah, Ahmed El-Sayed, and Ruland, William.
     "The Decision to Terminate Overfunded Pension Plans."
     Journal of Accounting & Public Policy 5 (Summer 1986):
     77-91.

983. Hawthorne, Fran. "Raiding the Corporate Pension
     Fund." Institutional Investor 17 (December 1983):
     101-113.

984. Ippolito, Richard A. "Pension Termination for Revi-
     sion." Journal of Pension Planning & Compliance 12
     (Fall 1986): 221-242.

985. Levin, Noel A., and Schelberg, Neal S. "Establishing
     a Plan Termination Date for Involuntary Terminations."
     Pension World 20 (January 1984): 43-44, 51.

986. Levin, Noel A., and Schelberg, Neal S. "Partial Plan
     Terminations: What Is a 'Significant Reduction' in Par-
     ticipations?" Pension World 20 (June 1984): 52-54.

987. Macris, Michael. "Partial Terminations of Qualified
     Plans." Journal of Pension Planning & Compliance 11
     (Spring 1985): 49-57.

988. Marcus, Alan J., and Merville, Larry. "Spinoff/Termi-
     nations and the Value of Pension Insurance/Discussion."
     Journal of Finance 40 (July 1985): 911-926.

989. Paustian, Chuck. "$10 Billion Is Recovered in Termi-
     nations." Pensions & Investment Age 14 (February 17,
     1986): 3, 82.

990. "Pension Expenses Dropping: J&H Study." National
     Underwriter Life and Health Insurance Edition 89
     (December 28, 1985): 2.

991.   Pension Fund Assets Revert to Employees." Business
        Insurance 20 (November 3, 1986): 36.

992.   Pianko, Howard. "Plan Termination and Asset Rever-
        sion." Journal of Pension Planning & Compliance 11
        (Winter 1985): 347-356.

993.   "Private Pension Plan Terminations." Social Security
        Bulletin 26 (December 1963): 18-21.

994.   Randolph, J. W. "Terminating an ERISA/PBGC Guaran-
        teed Pension Plan." Best's Review Property/Liability
        Edition 81 (December 1980): 29-30+.

995.   Ring, Trudy. "Twist in Terminations: Use of Hedging
        Strategies Could Be Catching On." Pensions & Invest-
        ment Age 14 (November 10, 1986): 77-78.

996.   Soucie, John E., and Kreiser, Larry. "Issues Surround-
        ing the Termination of Overfunded Defined Benefit
        Pension Plans." Ohio CPA Journal 46 (Winter 1987):
        27-33.

997.   "Terminating Well-Funded Defined Benefit Plans/Defined
        Contribution Plans Replacing Defined Benefits." Employee
        Benefit Plan Review 38 (July 1983): 26-30, 94-96.

998.   "Termination Rules Reflect Budget Act Changes."
        Employee Benefit Plan Review 42 (April 1988): 52-54.

GLOSSARY OF TERMS

Actuarial Assumptions: The assumed rates of wages, interest, pension inflation, and mortality used by the actuary to estimate the value of a pension plan.

Beneficiary: A person eligible for benefits under the terms of a plan.

Cash or Deferred Plan: A qualified profit-sharing or stock bonus plan that allows participants the option to withdraw cash or have their share of the employer contribution deposited into their respective plan.

Combination Plans: The use of two or more plans in combination to provide retirement benefits for employees and their beneficiaries.

Defined Benefit Plan: A pension plan stating the benefits to be received by employees after retirement or stating the method of determining such benefits. Contributions under such a plan are actuarially determined.

Defined Contribution Plan: A plan which provides an individual account for each participant. Benefits are based solely upon the amount contributed to the account. A profit-sharing plan is a good example of a defined contribution plan.

Employee Stock Ownership Plan (ESOP): A defined contribution pension plan which invests primarily in employer securities. Unlike other plans, an ESOP may borrow from the employer or use the employer's credit to acquire company stock.

ERISA: Employer Retirement Income Security Act of 1974. The basic law covering qualified pension plans; it includes pertinent labor law and Internal Revenue Code provisions.

ERTA: Economic Recovery Act of 1981. This act permits employed workers the right to establish individual retirement accounts and deduct contributions made to the account from their federal income tax.

Fiduciary: One who exercises discretionary authority or control over management of a plan or disposition of its assets, renders investment advice for a fee, or has authority or responsibility to do so, or has discretionary authority or responsibility in administering a plan.

Frozen Plan: A qualified pension or profit-sharing plan that continues to exist even though employer contributions have been discontinued and benefits are no longer accured by participants. The plan is frozen for purposes of distribution of benefits under the terms of the plan.

Integrated Plan: A plan that takes into account either benefits or contributions under Social Security. Social Security benefits are used to integrate a defined benefit plan while Social Security contributions are used with defined contribution plans.

Keogh Plan: A qualified retirement plan available to self-employed individuals and their employees. Annual tax deductible contributions of the lesser of 25 percent of income or $30,000 are permitted.

Master Plan: A retirement plan sponsored by a financial institution such as an insurance company, a bank, a mutual fund, or a stock brokerage firm, which can be adopted by an employer by executing a participation agreement.

Model Plans: Plans prepared by the Internal Revenue Service for small employers. Model plans are easy and inexpensive to implement due to the simple IRS procedure required for qualification.

Money Purchase Pension Plan: A defined contribution plan whereby employer contributions are mandatory and usually based on a participant's compensation. Retirement benefits are determined by the participant's individual account at retirement.

Multiemployer Plan: A plan maintained according to a

collective bargaining agreement which covers the employees
of more than one employer. An employee may change employers within the group without losing retirement benefits.
Employers within a group are not financially related but
are engaged in the same industry.

Noncontributory Plan: A pension plan whereby employees are
eligible to participate and receive accrued benefits without
contributing to the plan.

Pension Benefit Guaranty Corporation (PBGC): A nonprofit
federal body responsible for administering the plan termination insurance program under ERISA.

Pension Plan: A plan established and maintained by an
employer, group of employers, union, or any combination
thereof, for the purpose of providing the payment of
benefits to participants after retirement.

Profit-Sharing Plan: A defined contribution plan whereby
the employer agrees to make a contribution out of company
or corporate profits. A participant's retirement benefits
are based on the amount in his/her individual account at
retirement.

Qualified Plan: A plan which the Internal Revenue Service
approves as meeting the requirements of section 401(a)
of the 1954 Internal Revenue Code. Employers are per-
mitted, under the Code's provisions, to deduct contributions
to the plan for tax advantages.

Split Funded Plan: A plan that is funded in part by insurance
contracts and in part by funds accumulated in a separate
trusteed fund.

Target Benefit Plan: A cross between a defined benefit plan
and a money purchase plan. The annual contribution is
determined by the amount needed each year to fund a
targeted retirement benefit to each participant reaching
retirement age. Contributions are allocated to separate
accounts maintained for each participant.

TEFRA: Tax Equity and Fiscal Responsibility Act of 1982.
This act lowered the limits on contributions and benefits
for corporate plans. The real estate exclusion for retirement

plan death benefits was reduced to a maximum of $100,000, and "top heavy" plan requirements were also added.

Termination: This occurs when the sponsoring employer voluntarily terminates the plan or when the IRS makes a determination, due to an employers failure to make contributions, that the plan has been terminated.

"Top Heavy" Plan: A plan that primarily benefits key employees (i.e., a corporate officer, employee owning largest interest in the employer, a greater than 5 percent owner, a greater than one percent owner earning more than $150,000) and qualifies for favorable tax treatment by meeting regular and special qualification requirements.

Block, Robin S. 883
Bodie, Zvi 125, 179, 180, 397, 735
Borgmeyer, S. R. 253
Boyers, Judith T. 876
Boynton, E. F. 736
Bratter, H. 737
Brauer, Mary A. 254, 897
Brennan, Lawrence T. 121, 570
Brenner, George D. 255
Bret, William N. 398
Brinson, Gary P. 579, 580
Bristol, James T. 95, 181
Bronson, Dorrance C. 399
Brooks, John N. 581
Brooks, William A. 909
Brossman, Mark E. 901, 902
Brostoff, Steven 256
Brothers, D. I. 178
Brown, Betty C. 12
Brown, M. V. 257
Brownlee, E. Richard 13
Bruinsma, James C. 974
Bublitz, Bruce 83
Buckner, Kathryn C. 794, 884
Buppert, W. I. 400
Burianek, Frank 182, 401
Burke, Francis D. 936
Burkhauser, Richard V. 153
Burns, Gary W. 5
Burr, Barry B. 402, 582, 583
Burroughs, Eugene B. 162, 584, 585, 586, 587
Burrows, E. E. 738
Bush, Edwin M. 975
Bussewitz, Walter 739
Buxbaum, William E. 14, 15
Byland, Terry 258

Cahan, Vicky 588
Canada, Mark P. 937
Carberry Pauline R. 938
Carson-Parker, John 522
Casale, Debra A. 523

Cash, Doris C. 794, 884
Cashman, D. V. 589
Caswell, Jerry W. 547
Cerino, Ronald J. 259
Chadwick, G. R. 976
Chadwick, William J. 260
Chandor, Jeffrey F. 839
Chen, K. C. 971
Chia, Nelson P. 183
Christensen, Kenneth E. 16
Christiansen, Hanne D. 885
Christiansen, William A. 753
Christie, Claudia M. 590
Christman, Ed 143
Cirino, R. 505
Clark, Arben O. 154
Clark, Robert L. 403
Clay, William L. 261
Cleary, William T. 404
Cleveland, M. G. 165
Cochran, J. R. 741
Cogan, Bruce A. 883
Cohen, Cynthia F. 96
Cohen, Sheryl L. 17, 69
Cohn, Richard A. 591
Cole, Rebel 840
Collins, Adrian A. 262
Connors, J. A. 405
Conrad, A. 592
Cook, Thomas J. 97
Cooke, James A. 263
Cooper, Robert D. 184, 264, 406, 524
Coppage, Richard E. 12
Corpus, Janet M. 742
Costa, Michael L. 407
Cottle, Sidney 506, 593
Covaleski, John 408
Cozort, Larry A. 485
Crabbe, Matthew 594
Cramer, Joe J. 19
Crawford, Diane 409
Crichton, J. H. 265
Croot, D. J. 185
Cropsey, Betsy H. 20

Author Index

132 Pension Funds

Kilberg, William J. 310
King, Francis P. 196
Kittrell, Alison 103, 133, 812
Klein, James P. 542
Klein, John R. 48
Klimkowsky, Beverly M. 311
Kline, Allan M. 49
Knowles, Bob 442
Knox, Peter L. 312
Koeblitz, William M. 67
Kogovsek, Raymond P. 813
Kolodrubetz, W. W. 204, 764
Kopp, B. 649
Kopp, B. S. 650
Kossak, Shelley E. 792
Kostolansky, John W. 91, 386
Kraabel, Stephen E. 443
Krass, Stephen J. 879
Krauss, Alan 444, 651, 855
Kreiser, L. 50, 996
Kritzman, Mark 652
Krueger, James M. 814
Kutz, Karen S. 497

Laing, Jonathon R. 515
Laketek, Maryann 104
Lampf, S. E. 948
Landau, Peter 516
Landen, R. W. 765
Landsman, Wayne 51, 313
Lang, Larry 134, 445
Langetieg, T. C. 314
Lanoff, Ian D. 315, 316, 900
Lashgari, Malek K. 591
Lavin, William K. 52
Lawler, Kathy A. 486
Leaton, Edward K. 317
Leavit, Thomas D. 116
Lechner, Melvin N. 815
Ledolter, Johannes 766
Lehman, June M. 816
Lehrer, Brian 817, 915
Leibig, Michael T. 205, 818
Leibowitz, Martin L. 654, 655

Leo, Mario 767
Lerner, Eugene M. 656
Levin, Noel A. 901, 902, 985, 986
Liebtag, Bill 53
Lindbeck, R. S. 572
Lindquist, J. R. 318
Lipkin, David M. 532
Litvak, Lawrence 206, 657
LoCicero, Joseph A. 319, 487
Lofgren, Eric P. 658
Logue, Dennis E. 135, 446
Lohrer, Richard B. 447
Lowa, R. J. 949
Lucas, Timothy S. 54
Luris, Alvin D. 320

MacKiewicz, Edward R. 284
Mackin, John P. 819
Macris, Michael 987
Mactas, L. 768
Madden, William B. 448
Mahar, Maggie 561
Mahoney, M. J. 736
Main, J. 207
Mainer, R. E. 410
Mainer, Robert 449
Malca, Edward 659, 660
Maldonado, K. F. 450, 950
Malecki, Donald S. 451
Malley, Susan L. 321, 661
Malmon, A. S. 55
Maloney, Elizabeth 56
Mamorsky, Jeffrey D. 163, 165, 166, 322, 323, 452
Manson, William D. 954
Mara, Rod 136
Marcus, Alan J. 988
Mares, Judith W. 903
Margady, Myles 453
Margel, Lawrence N. 76
Margolin, Stephen M. 951
Margotta, Donald 662